MAN & BEAST

MAN & BEAST

Andrew Rule

MELBOURNE
UNIVERSITY
PRESS

RICH

MELBOURNE UNIVERSITY PRESS
An imprint of Melbourne University Publishing Limited
Level 1, 715 Swanston Street, Carlton, Victoria 3053, Australia
mup-info@unimelb.edu.au
www.mup.com.au

First published 2016
Text © individual contributors, 2016
Design and typography © Melbourne University Publishing Limited, 2016

Phillip Adams' 'Lassie' was first published in *Adams' Ark: Dogs, Frogs, Roos, Bulls and
    Other Memorable Animals*, Penguin, 2004
Les Carlyon's 'The Horse Whisperer' was first published in *The Sunday Age* and the
    Sun-Herald, 26 January 1997
Robert Drewe's 'Masculine Shoes' was first published in *The Rip*, Penguin, 2008
Jonathan Green's 'Rein Lover' was first published in *The Age*, 2006
Garry Linnell's 'Stud' is an edited version of longer piece published as 'Stand and Deliver'
    in *Good Weekend* on 2 November 2002
Frank Robson's 'Lucky' was first published (as 'Lucky's Last Voyage') in *Good Weekend*
    magazine, March 2012
Andrew Rule's 'Kid on a Crock' was first published (as 'Dream Ride') in *The Sunday Age*,
    3 November 1996
John Silvester's 'Animal Acts' was first published in *The Age*, July 2016
Paul Toohey's 'Roo Dogs' was first published in *The Bulletin*, September 2006
Don Watson's 'Society of Birds' was first published in *The Monthly*, Christmas
    edition, 2007; the extract from 'Birds' by Judith Wright, is reproduced with permission
    of HarperCollins Publishers Australia and New Zealand © Judith Wright Estate

Cover design by Philip Campbell Design
Typeset by Megan Ellis
Printed in Australia by Ligare

National Library of Australia Cataloguing-in-Publication entry
Rule, Andrew, 1957– author.
Man and beast/Andrew Rule.

9780522870879 (paperback)
9780522870886 (ebook)

Human–animal relationships—Australia.
Animals—Australia—Anecdotes.
Animals—Social aspects—Australia.

304.270994

For Sweetie

Contents

Andrew Rule
Animal Kingdom   1

Phillip Adams
Lassie   7

Greg Baum
Four Legs Bad   15

Tony Birch
Mustang Sally   21

John Birmingham
Dirty Dog   27

Anson Cameron
Snake Dog   31

Les Carlyon
The Horse Whisperer   37

John Clarke
Bird Brains   49

Greg Combet
Man and Bird   53

Trent Dalton
Acrocalypse Now   59

Robert Drewe
Masculine Shoes   65

John Elder
Cat and Moustache   77

Jonathan Green
Rein Lover   87

John Harms
Island Bream   95

Malcolm Knox
Rescue Dog   101

Garry Linnell
Stud   111

William McInnes
Shepherds   117

Shaun Micallef
A Boy and His Dog   123

Bruce Pascoe
Smiling in the Dark   131

Liam Pieper
Cat Lovers   137

Frank Robson
Lucky   145

Andrew Rule
Kid on a Crock   149

John Silvester
Animal Acts   157

Jeff Sparrow
Mimi and Rosa   163

Paul Toohey
Roo Dogs   171

Don Watson
Society of Birds   177

Tony Wilson
Epsilon   185

Tony Wright
Gee Gee v GG   193

Biographies   199

Animal Kingdom

Andrew Rule

All his life he hated swimming and liked animals. He had his reasons.

A dog had saved him once when he was running away from a hard-hearted pig farmer, a distant relative who remembered to work the homeless boy seven days a week but forgot to pay him.

He told us the story nearly seventy years later, the way old men do when they realise the past means more than their future.

His absent father, a gambling man, had shunted him from family to family after his mother had died in childbirth in the early 1890s. So it was early in the new century that he was working in East Gippsland for the relative, name of McDiarmid, on the promise of a small wage that was never paid. What he got instead was hard work, bad food, a makeshift bunk in a shed and the constant threat of a hiding.

He seethed quietly for months. When he finally confronted the farmer about the missing pay, he was told he wouldn't be getting any. And what was he going to do about it?

The boy had nowhere to go but he went anyway, bolting west through paddocks and bush, the injustice burning his brain, fear driving his feet. He was striking out for the Stratford district, avoiding roads and bridges where he might be seen. By chance, a working dog followed, a big, rangy thing he'd befriended on the farm.

He struck the swamps the locals called 'the Morass'. In wet years the streams feeding Lake Wellington spilled over and filled a maze of creeks, billabongs and reed beds, ideal for ducks and snakes but not for the runaway boy.

He thought he could wade across one lonely stretch of water but it was deceptive. He was soon out of his depth and had to swim or turn back. His clothes weighed him down and he was tired and terrified of drowning. He could hardly dog paddle but his four-legged mate could. As he started to struggle and panic, the dog jumped in and swam to him.

He grabbed its collar and held on. It was a strong dog. Strong enough to get him to the far side and a long, cold walk into an uncertain future.

No one alive knows what that dog looked like or his name, if he had one. It must have turned for home when it got hungry but the boy couldn't. The swamp was his Rubicon. He'd burned his bridges.

That boy's name was Len Rule and a lifetime later he would become my grandfather.

Somehow he survived, scraping a living working for farmers and contractors. One Saturday he got hold of a pony to ride to a race meeting at Stratford, a sleepy little town where the highway and the railway line bridge the Avon River near Sale.

He was worried that McDiarmid or the police might catch up with him, so he planted the pony, saddled and bridled, in a clump of trees near the course, ready for a fast getaway if things went wrong. It sounded like something out of *Robbery under Arms* but there was no dramatic punchline, no chase.

Nothing bad happened that day. But it did soon enough, after Len joined his older brother Ernie on the other side of the ranges. On Boxing Day 1904, the brothers went to the races run by the publican at Buxton, in the hills between Marysville and Alexandra.

Ernie, who was sixteen, rode in four races that day. He placed in the first three. In the fourth, his mount, Cronje, fell and Ernie suffered what *The Argus* reported the next day as 'terrible injuries to the head'. A local newspaper reported nonchalantly that the Buxton racecourse was 'rather rough' and had caused several bad falls but that the musical entertainment after the race meeting was enjoyed by all.

As the revelry began, Len was in a dray taking his unconscious brother on the agonising trip to hospital at Alexandra. Ernie died the next morning. At thirteen, Len was now the oldest of two survivors of six children.

His world was cruel but he never was, to man or beast.

He lived in the machine age and saw the space age begin but never quite embraced them. Until the day he died (peacefully, after an afternoon spent rounding up sheep on a pony called Scout) he oiled his old harness in the shed as if the internal combustion motor might prove a temporary fad and he'd be back to real horsepower, the four-legged sort. He couldn't cut the tie with the past and the animals he knew there.

Even those we were too young to remember, he spoke of so fondly it was as if we knew them, too. There was Peggy, the wise and kind Alsatian bitch that looked after his little children, my father and aunt. And the bay hack he called Plum 'because he was such a peach of a horse'.

Behind me as I type this is a picture of him holding two grey ponies on a far-off morning long before I was born. Their names were Bluey and Sonny. There's another picture of my father as a nine year old on Bluey, holding his baby cousin in front of the saddle.

Len was a 'soft touch' to the end, rescuing a tough old black dog—we called him Bill—he'd found limping along the road. Probably a handy dog that fell from a stock truck, the old man would assert, as if answering an unasked question about why he'd feed a stray for years.

He bought a plain old thoroughbred mare with a split hoof from the killer pens at Bairnsdale horse sale, and surprised everyone except himself by breeding a slashing colt out of her, such a fine type it went on to win Supreme Champion stallion at Melbourne Royal the year after the old man died.

Just short of eighty, he had handled that big colt so well that when my cousin the horseman jumped on him the first time, the horse went so easily a kid could ride him out of the yard half an hour later. I was the kid, King Arthur on his charger.

Ancient instincts linger, making us fond of our fellow creatures in ways that defy cold logic. Our caveman ancestors first tamed fire, then tamed the wild forebears of our sleek domestic breeds. Surely that's why it's so deeply satisfying to sit in front of a fire with a dog or cat—at some level we are back in the cave, the sense of shared warmth and safety imprinted in man and beast.

....

Once, in Cambodia, I met a man whose family had been murdered in Pol Pot's killing fields. His parents had been educated city people, doomed to die under the dictator's mad plan for a peasant society. They smuggled their little son to peasant cousins in the provinces, hoping he at least could fool the Khmer Rouge killers.

The boy saw terrible things. His own relatives did terrible things to survive, turning on neighbours and watching as innocent people were slaughtered—in fact, he would much later give evidence at war crimes trials at The Hague. Long after the holocaust he became a tourist guide, a multilingual gun for hire who made money and built a successful life in the place where his family was butchered.

We travelled with him for days but he did not share his story until the last few hours. He spoke evenly of the murder and torture, like the cool witness he had been. Then he talked of toiling in the paddy fields with a water buffalo he'd seen as his only 'friend', a living creature he could talk to that would not betray him.

He was a streetwise and worldly man, a survivor in an unsentimental society. But his face softened and his voice quavered as he described the beast of burden the frightened boy had used to plough the rice paddies thirty years before.

'I loved that buffalo,' he said, tears springing in his eyes.

Of course, the buffalo didn't really love him. As several writers in this collection point out, our relationship with animals is real but it is one-sided. *We* provide food, shelter and affection. Animals are expert at doing what it takes to keep up the supply.

Still, there's a bit of the water-buffalo boy in most of us. It's a hard heart that hasn't fallen for an animal some time.

That's why a middle-aged man, now a grandfather himself, sits down in a city skyscraper at the start of every working day and taps out the name of a pony mare he had half a century ago.

Her name was Amber and it's the only login I can remember.

Lassie

Phillip Adams

'Near this spot are deposited the remains of one who possessed
beauty without vanity, strength without insolence, courage without
ferocity, and all the virtues of man without his vices. This praise,
which would be unmeaning flattery if inscribed over human ashes,
is but a tribute to the memory of Boatswain, a dog.'

Byron (epitaph for a dog buried at Newstead Abbey)

'Whotsyer dog's name?'

That was an embarrassing question to a self-conscious
thirteen year old. My dog was a funny old thing, an ecumenical
merger of cocker, foxy, heeler, you name it. The tail should have
been a little shorter and the legs a lot longer, but she had a nice
face. And just as working-class mums often lumbered their
daughters with the names of movie stars, which served only
to emphasise their stoic lack of glamour, a previous owner had
called her Lassie.

'Lassie,' I'd mumble.

'Lassie! You call *that* Lassie!'

Actually I hadn't called her Lassie. She just *was* Lassie.
A second-hand dog, a used dog, a hand-me-down dog, she came
with a name. Just as she came with a collar, a length of chain and

a small crate that served as a kennel. She'd been offered to me by a departing neighbour, a bloke simply known as 'the English migrant', who'd lived in a larger crate, a crate that had contained an imported English car. A crate that had 'Humber' stencilled on it. He'd plonked it on his block of land and put a bed in it, ignoring the complaints of neighbours and the local council.

He claimed to be getting round to building a proper house but, finally, changed his mind. After a couple of years he left the big crate and went back to England, leaving me the little crate, with the dog. The English migrant's name was Bruce. Hers was Lassie.

I resented the poor old dog for not being a sleek, long-legged collie, and would have preferred to have a male dog I could have called Bluey. And when I apologised for her, she'd look up with eyes full of love, making me feel tawdry and disloyal.

I'd wanted a dog all right, something spectacular to lope beside my bike as I pedalled the 4 dusty miles to school, to play Cheetah to my Tarzan when I went Weissmullering in the scrub. When the setters or Alsatians weren't forthcoming, I'd settled for Lassie.

Lassie was no puppy, so she fretted for a while. I'd find her down the road, whimpering by the 'Humber' crate. Yet when the dog finally resigned herself to her new fate, she gave me her total commitment. Half a century on, I remember that devotion with wonderment and pain.

I was ten years old when my mother decided it was time for me to live with her again. For the first time since I was two. She'd long since divorced my father, who, returning from the war, had gone back to the Congregational church as a local minister only to be dismissed from the posting because of a mixture of insubordination and alcohol. My mother had married again, and living with my stepfather was like being trapped in a horror film. When he wasn't threatening me with an axe, he was trying to run me down in his big black Studebaker. Or he'd pull all the fuses from the box and walk around the darkened house brandishing a rifle. Outbursts like this were comparatively welcome; moments of catharsis to punctuate something far more soul destroying—his constant abuse of both me and my mother. Years of tension and trauma had their effect, turning me into a lonely, alienated kid, who, exiled in his bedroom, spent most of his time reading and writing. Except when attacks on Mum forced me to try to fight him. The day we moved into the house, surrounded by empty paddocks, in Briar Hill, there was such a fight. When he lunged at my mother I somehow managed to hurl him across a double bed into the venetian blinds—which would, forever after, bear his imprint.

So I read hundreds of books borrowed from the local library and filled cardboard boxes with scraps of short stories and ideas for novels. The result was a thirteen year old entirely lacking in social competence, whose shortage of schoolfriends made his need for a dog all the more intense.

'Have you got that rotten dog in there?'

'No, Pop.' I refused to call him Dad. Even 'Pop' outraged my sense of decency and justice. But it had been a negotiated sentiment, to make things easier for my mother.

Lassie was, of course, under the bed. She became very good at hiding.

Every morning she'd run beside me, detouring to chase sheep or magpies. At school she became very popular because of her ability to field cricket balls and, for a time, I enjoyed some reflected glory. She'd sit outside the classroom, stealthily returning after the caretaker had chased her away. And at lunchtime, I'd see her darting and sniffing among hundreds of uniformed kids, looking for me. Then it was a moment of rapture and she'd trot behind me to the quince orchard to share my sandwiches. I'd eat the centres, she'd eat the crusts.

'Adams, you *must* stop bringing that dog to school,' the head-master would say, but without much heat. In the end she was accepted, marching behind me around the oval in those weekly ceremonials, snapping at footballs, chasing the magpies from the dustbins.

After school, some of us would climb into the hills and go swimming in a big dam in an area where some of Eltham's artists—painters, sculptors and potters—lived in their mudbrick houses. Here Lassie would go berserk. As soon as I dived in the water she'd follow, desperately trying to save me. She'd take my hand or foot in her mouth and, flailing in the water, try to pull me back to the shore. And when I was out she'd set about licking me dry, convinced that this sizeable child was her puppy.

Once a month, on a Friday night, I'd be allowed to walk the 3 miles to the Greensborough pictures, a tiny cinema in the shopping centre, holding about 100 in acute discomfort. On these occasions I'd command her to 'Stay home'. And I'd meet Carl Andrew, my only friend at school, and we'd talk about not believing in God and how logical communism was, and we'd hike to see some wretched Esther Williams movie, or Doris Day in *Calamity Jane*.

After one such Friday, I returned home to find that Lassie was missing. All Saturday I searched for her, riding my bike up and down the eroded gullies that passed for roads on the outskirts of Eltham. It wasn't until Sunday night, hoarse from calling, that I suddenly knew where she was. Keeping out of sight so I wouldn't yell at her, she'd followed me to the pictures, so I was looking for her in the wrong place. I rode my bike into town and, yes, Lassie was sitting outside the cinema. I can still see her, on the deserted footpath, looking at the shuttered doors with patient expectancy.

All too often, and to my eternal shame, her reward for this sort of loyalty was a hiding. It's often the lot of a dog to cop the kicks received by its master. Most of the time we clung together, united in our hatred of our uncommon enemy, the deranged man who'd suddenly throw a bucket of water on the fire I'd lit for Mum, or who'd suddenly appear on the platform of Greensborough station, pulling me from the carriage when I was on my way to visit my real father, scattering the contents of my suitcase under everybody's feet.

But there were times when I was so tormented by his bullying and sadism that I'd take it out on Lassie and thump her until I was exhausted and weeping. And then she'd come quivering to me and lick my face, shaming me with the sort of understanding you'd expect from some beatified paragon. And we'd huddle together, me begging her for the forgiveness she'd already given.

Lassie's saintliness recalls the arguments I'd have with our religious instruction teacher, who regarded my insistence on her having a soul as blasphemy. But I knew she did, that she must, and that if there were a heaven and heavenly justice, she'd have to share in immortality. 'No,' he'd say, 'dogs do not have human understanding. They do not know about good and evil.' 'Not much she doesn't,' I'd protest. 'She feels all of the emotions you do—happiness, sadness, love, fear, compassion.' And he'd get angrier and the kids would flick wads of blotting paper at him. Yet I was entirely serious. Lassie had more sensitivity and understanding than almost anyone I knew. And in the unlikely event of there being a God, He'd know that I was right.

'God is dog backwards,' offered Graeme Wrigley helpfully, only to earn instant excommunication from the class.

I don't know whether Lassie was special, as she's the only dog I ever had, ever knew. She could understand dozens and dozens of commands, comprehending the words, not just the tone of voice. (I would try to trick her by saying the words in different ways, but she always knew.) More than that, she had compassion—so that any theology that failed to encompass Lassie seemed absurdly inadequate.

Although my stepfather was a prominent KCC (Kennels Control Council) dog judge, always going off to agricultural shows to choose the Best Cocker Spaniel and the Best Bitch in Show, he disliked dogs as much as he did people. Even then, as a boy, I was sufficiently objective to realise that his cruelties must have been the product of great torment in his own childhood. But there was little consolation in that awareness when he was exacting vengeance. Inevitably, my closeness to that bloody dog infuriated him, and he was always making threats about getting rid of her. Not that he dared to try. I think Mum and I would have killed him first.

Yet, finally, he did find a way to punish us both, Lassie and me. She'd just had pups (the father was a big black dog who also hung around the high school) and I'd watched them both being born with a mixture of horror and awe. I'd spend hours on end with them, watching Lassie lick those blind faces, me tickling their tummies and ensuring that everyone got a feed.

And at the end of the week, I was ordered to drown them. No, nobody round here would want them. No, we wouldn't waste money putting an ad in the paper. Just pop the bloody things in this sack and take them down to the creek.

Because I couldn't let him see my anguish, because I wouldn't let myself beg, I took the puppies from Lassie, who looked at me with puzzlement and trust, and, having locked her in the garage, walked the mile to the creek. And all the time they wriggled and whimpered in the bag.

The reason I've written this recollection of a dog is because the horror of that day recently returned to me, undiminished. I found myself driving by what subdivisions had left of the creek. I was a child again, sitting on the bank, crooning to the puppies as they crawled and tumbled in my lap. And once again there was nothing I could do but push them back into the sack, retie it and hurl it into the deepest water. Once again, I remembered my pledge to murder the man who'd sent me there.

When I got home I couldn't look at Lassie. When she came up and licked my hand I couldn't bear it. Thanks to my stepfather I could never be as close to Lassie again. Two years later I got a five-dollar-a-week job and left home for the city. My guilt at leaving Lassie was as intense as my guilt at drowning her puppies—so intense that my memory has kindly clouded the issues, so that I can't quite remember what became of her. I think that Mum gave her to a neighbour's kids and hoped that things worked out all right. But perhaps I've made that up, in expiation.

The same day I passed the creek, I drove through the Greensborough shopping centre. There's a supermarket where the cinema used to be, yet Lassie was still sitting on the footpath, looking like the trademark for His Master's Voice. And when I drove through the school grounds of Eltham High, there she was, chasing cricket balls on the oval.

My religious instruction teacher is now in orbit high over Eltham, enjoying his eternal rewards. And if I'm right, his pleasures in heaven will be marred by the faintly blasphemous presence of my ecumenical dog, chasing the cricket balls.

Four Legs Bad

Greg Baum

Man, wake up. This idea that a dog is your best friend: you've been had. The time has come for man to unfriend dogs.

Dogs aren't the cute and clever creatures they seem on the internet, or in other people's photos, or your own, for that matter. They bark, mewl, growl, drool, lick—lick!—slobber, sniff, gnaw, paw and nuzzle. Nuzzling might seem innocent enough, but I can never get out of my mind where that nose last was. Dogs cannot resist other dogs' anuses. They fart, spray and shit in random places, and expect you to pick it up. Humans don't do that. Not all of them.

Dogs bite, and think it's play. They eat things. One in our house tried to eat a chair. They leave toothmarks everywhere. And did I mention shit? Right where you are likely to walk next. Stepping on a dog turd is like getting hit in the groin in cricket: everyone thinks it's funny when it happens to someone else. It's not.

Dogs leave detritus strewn all over the house and garden. So do babies and teenagers and some relatives, but at least when you bellow at them to pick it up, they do, however grudgingly. A dog just sits there and fixes you with a silly grin.

Dogs eat holes in underwear. Dogs eat holes in overwear. Dogs eat holes everywhere. As if it isn't hard enough to keep a pair of socks together in the first place.

Dogs destroy perfectly good tennis balls, until they are unusable for backyard cricket. Otherwise, they field in backyard cricket, which so misses the point. There's little enough to do anyway without outsourcing one function to a mutt.

Dogs are devious. They tear a book to shreds, or a T-shirt, or a couch, then sit there with a calculatedly dopey look on their face, knowing you're probably going to pull out your smartphone and post it all over the internet. That's another thing: they've ruined Facebook.

They sit. Like, wow!

Dogs are supposed to be smart, but cats are clearly smarter, by a long way. Cats aren't anyone's best friend; they just let you think it from time to time, for strategic purposes. Dogs might have goldfish covered, although how would you know?

Dogs smell, but do nothing about it. You wash them, they protest and then start smelling again, immediately.

They hate clean, hot water. But any other sort of water, they plunge into it, and leap out of it, and shake themselves and the spray goes everywhere. The only thing worse than a dog is a wet dog.

They grow. Or they don't. Almost none of them is the right size. Either they trip up under your feet or they leap upon you and try to flatten you. If they succeed, they lick you. If they don't, they try again. They do this even to complete strangers. If a human 'friend' did any of these things, they would be reported to the authorities, compulsorily. Dogs are patted for it, which means that they do it all again, of course.

They are loyal? They love you unconditionally? I don't think so. Watch how quickly a dog moves on to the next feeder/patter/walker/coochie-coochie-coo-er/more interesting-smelling anus if you don't provide.

They have to walk or they go crazy, but if you do walk them, they constantly tangle up the lead and you go crazy.

If you walk for exercise, they take you on needless detours. If you walk for recreation, they take you on needless detours. I'd rather walk with my own thoughts. Granted, those can be a bit scatty and undisciplined, too, which is why I don't need a dog to try to control as well.

Walking dogs breaks down social barriers? Excuse me, telling a complete stranger that her dog is gorgeous, guessing the breed and banging your head when you get it wrong does not constitute socialisation. Might as well just sniff each other's bums.

Dogs shed, and malt, and get fleas, and scratch themselves in public. They dig holes, which would be OK if they then put their poo in them, but they don't.

They dig up whole gardens, then trample the mud through the house, and expect you to love them for it. Or at least give them a biscuit.

They howl for your attention just as the footy gets interesting, or as your favourite miniseries reaches a crucial point. They interrupt everything: phone calls, meals, conversations, reading, coitus. Some things are unforgivable.

They go to puppy school, but don't learn anything. They get a pass anyway, and you get a bill. They go to obedience school and don't get much past 'sit', and you get another bill anyway.

Dogs run up bills: food, shelter, vet, sundry toys, council, grooming, holiday accommodation, legal fees, cleaning agents.

Counselling.

Dogs confound holiday plans. If you can't take them with you, you have to make provisions. If you can take them with you, you have to make provisions.

Dogs scare kids. I've seen this, often. They scare adults: I'm one.

Their owners expect you to admire them, and not to notice their snub noses, pushed-in faces, stumpy legs, ridiculous hair, misshapen ears, roly-poly shape, gimpy gait or patches of missing fur. Or that they're really, really fat. In this, dogs are worse than babies.

Worse than all this, they'll turn your real friends into blithering idiots who somehow think it's amazing when their dog runs and fetches and brings back a stick they just threw.

And knows its own name.

Dogs reduce intelligent humans to the level of infants, calling out unintelligible non-words in high, non-natural voices. Somehow, dogs think that these are endearments.

Dogs have to be replaced, more often than humans. Yet we keep replacing them, knowing how it will all end. I'm not going to say outright that Koreans have the right idea, but let's face it: we eat lots of other creatures and think nothing of it.

I'll concede this much: bulldogs. I read that they sleep twenty-two hours a day. That sounds friendly. I could negotiate around that.

But who appointed dogs as man's best friend, anyway? On what basis? What about, say, horses? Horses have served man so well for so long in all sorts of ways, yet only dogs are called man's best friend. Chickens have been right there, too. Then again, who wants to be the best friend of a species that calls dogs its best friend?

OK, dogs rescue souls lost in deep snowdrifts in alpine blizzards, but, frankly, there's not much call for that my way. They round up sheep, but that hardly constitutes an argument for *amigos para siempre*, or else trail bikes would have to be considered, too. Dogs sit for hours by their critically injured masters, but wouldn't it be a whole lot more useful if they could administer first aid, or make a phone call? If a real best friend sat there doing nothing other than lick you while you slowly lost consciousness, he wouldn't be your best friend for long. Dogs sound the alert at a break-in, but so does an alarm system, and it doesn't evacuate its bowels on the back doorstep twice a day.

This leads to the really delicate part. I have this hunch that some people love dogs because dog-love gives them the sort of mastery in a relationship that they could never have over another human being. It's about dependence, and the power that comes with it. Loving, yes, but the lines of control are clear. Dog owners I've run this past protest a little too vehemently for me not to be even more suspicious. The saddest thing is that even on those terms, it doesn't always work out.

Maybe I've just been lucky, but I've always had a set of human friends who provide all the nourishment on all the levels I need, and don't commit any of the foregoing atrocities, not often anyway, and if they ever do, at least we can talk about it. It hasn't always been easy, but it's worked much better for me than the naughty corner in the bad times and a biscuit in the good and a lot of goofy-eyed, smelly-breathed face licking in between.

I know that in my position on dogs, I'm in a tiny minority. I'm happy there.

Mustang Sally

Tony Birch

When my uncle, Michael, was sixteen years old he spent a year in a youth detention centre after being convicted of a break and enter at a factory in Collingwood. I would visit him with my mother occasionally, walking from our home in Fitzroy to the Turana Boys Home in Parkville. I loved my uncle. He was a sweet-faced kid and he and my mother were close. He was the second youngest of eight children and she was particularly protective of him. Some said that Michael was *slow*, but I think he was a dreamer. I was only five years old during the time of those weekend visits and could not quite understand that each time we left the home my uncle could not come with us. When the time came for his release, Michael came to live with us. Our home was already overcrowded. My parents shared the front room of the house with the lounge suite, the television and the fireplace, and I slept in the second room with two brothers and two sisters.

My father dominated that small house with his physical presence, his sullen moods and unpredictable explosiveness. Michael arrived with his only belongings in a battered suitcase, consisting of a few items of spare clothes, a breadboard that he had made for my mother in the home and a few comic books. I moved into a bottom bunk with my older brother; Michael took the top bunk. He settled in, got a job in a factory around the corner, and changed the tone of the house with his laughter, practical jokes and storytelling, which filled the bedroom long after the lights were put out for the night.

If one new arrival in the house tested my father, two had the potential to send him into a rage. About a month after Michael moved in I was sent around the corner to Brunswick Street one Saturday morning with my older sister, Deborah, to do the shopping for my mother. My sister went into the butcher's and I stood outside, looking in the window at the cuts of meat. I felt something licking the side of my leg and looked down to see a dog. She was brown with white socks on all four feet. After I gave her a pat she ran around me in circles, wagging her tail wildly. When Deborah came out of the shop we began walking home. The dog followed us, first at a distance, but as soon as we'd turned the corner, she caught up and ran around me excitedly. My sister tried shooing her away, without success. The she unwrapped the parcel, took out a chop, waved it in front of the dog's face then hurled it as far as she could. The dog ran after the chop, sniffed at it for a moment and bit into it.

By the time we'd turned into our street the dog was back for more. She followed us home to our front gate. Several times in the past we'd asked my father if we could have a dog. In those days puppies were given away free. Sometimes a box full of pups would be left outside the corner shop for anybody who wanted one. My father had always said no, telling us he could hardly afford to feed his own kids let alone a dog.

He was sleeping off a hangover that Saturday morning and I managed to sneak out of the house with another chop, without being discovered. The dog and I spent the day on *'the flat'*, a scrubby piece of land behind Young Street, Fitzroy, where kids played marbles, British Bulldog and learned to smoke cigarettes. By the late afternoon, when it was time to go home, I wasn't sure what to do with the dog. In the end I let her follow me and snuck her into the house by the side gate. I tried coaxing her into the toilet in the corner of the yard, where I planned to hide her. She was too smart to allow herself to be locked up and sprinted around the yard in wide circles, as if I were a sheep she was rounding up. She barked at me so loudly that my mother came out of the kitchen. She pointed and screamed *a dog!* Michael wasn't far behind her. He smiled, ran to the dog and tickled her behind an ear. She jumped up at him, barked again and licked his face. My mother looked at me ominously and walked back into the house, leaving Michael and me to play with the dog until sundown.

We could set the clock by my father's pub hours. He got home exactly ten minutes after six o'clock closing time. The dog was in the yard. I began to pray that she would keep quiet at least until my father fell asleep in front of the fire, which he always did. My mother cooked chops that night and the dog smelled them as they were being dished up at the table. She barked, yelped and scratched at the back door. My father jumped up from the table, pulled the door open and screamed *what the fuck is this!* My brothers and sisters ran into the yard, screaming with delight, and gathered around the dog. I looked up at my mother's face and saw her look of fear.

In any other circumstances my father would have kicked the dog up the arse and thrown it into the street. But Michael came to the rescue. He saved me, my mother and the dog. He told my father the animal belonged to him. When my father delivered his usual complaint that we couldn't afford to feed it, Michael assured him that he'd pay for the dog's food from his own money, he'd pick up her shit in the yard and make sure she wouldn't be a nuisance. We looked at my father for a response but got none. He walked back into the house, defeated for one of the few times during my childhood.

We enjoyed the summer with Sally, the name Deborah gave the dog. She followed me everywhere I went during the day, and at night I would sneak her into our room, where she'd sleep until morning. My father worked for the local council and left the house early. Once he'd gone I let the dog out in the street. She'd go off on her own to explore before returning to the house for breakfast, which consisted of a bowl of milky tea and two slices of buttered toast. The only problem with Sally was that generally she didn't like men, including my father. Michael was about to turn eighteen, but with his baby-faced looks and sense of innocence, Sally treated him as just another kid.

One night during the following winter I was lying in bed when I heard a knock at the front door. Sally let out a low growl. At first I thought it was Michael. He hadn't come home from work and I assumed he'd been locked out of the house. A few minutes later I heard voices in the next room, a loud scream and then sobbing. Thinking it was another of the many nights of fighting between my parents I put a pillow over my head, blocked my ears and fell asleep. The next morning, I woke to find my grandmother and several of my aunties and uncles in the kitchen drinking tea. Michael had been murdered the night before after he got into a fight in a laneway behind the Rainbow Hotel in Fitzroy. He was shot through the heart. It made little sense to me then, and makes less now, more than fifty years later.

The days after Michael's death remain a blur. But I do remember my mother found it difficult to get out of bed, and my father went to the pub and got drunk, as he usually did. Weeks after his funeral, with my sister Deborah taking me by the hand, Sally and I walked through the streets in the rain and stopped outside the laneway where Michael had been killed. I was a good Catholic in those days, an altar boy at the local church, All Saints, and a *believer*. I looked down at the bluestone pavers and wondered where Michael could be. Sally sniffed the air but wouldn't enter the lane. Decades later I published one of my first poems, *Michael*. It ended with the following stanza:

> And sometimes we walk
> along that laneway behind
> the Rainbow Hotel
> I look down for you
> and listen for the whistle
> of a bullet.

After Michael's death it was up to me to pay for Sally's keep from the money I made as a paper boy. I didn't mind. Sally had a litter of pups after a wild night out with a stray mongrel and we would keep the runt of the litter, Rusty, for the next twelve years.

Sally increasingly found herself in trouble on the street. When a debt collector turned up at the front door demanding money from my mother, she bit him on the calf. And when he came back a week later with a bill for the 'invisible mending' required for the hole in his suit pants, she bit him again. The next day a policeman came to the house riding a black bicycle. He picked up a broom and chased Sally around the yard with it. He eventually backed her into a corner, broke the broom handle across her back and proceeded to give her what my father would have termed *a good kicking*. Sally was a slow learner when it came to male authority. A few weeks later I was coming home from the street with her. It was getting dark, I was late and began to run. I turned the corner into our street and ran into a Salvation Army major. He'd been giving out prayer cards and collecting donations. He spooked

Sally and she responded by taking a chunk of meat out of his forearm. We ran home, the major following with a bloodied arm.

The next day the police returned, with a caged van and a net. Sally put up a good fight. It took the police fifteen minutes to net her. And she continued fighting, barking, snapping and tearing at the net with her claws until she was in the back of the van. One policeman laughed and winked at me before getting into the van and driving off. When I asked my mother where Sally was going she told me she was being sent to a holiday farm. I didn't believe a word of what she said but I understood why she said it and didn't hold it against her.

Dirty Dog

John Birmingham

I took the dog down to the beach, as is my wont. Once or twice a year we sojourn to Byron Bay. There's a Mexican joint there at the top of the main street that does excellent margaritas. This alone is reason enough to visit but the main purpose of driving for a couple of hours is to walk the dog.

The local government authorities maintain a relaxed attitude on the question of hounds set loose upon their sands. Most beachside local government authorities are implacably opposed to allowing dogs anywhere near the beach, but Byron, being in the thrall of Greens and vegans and winged fairies, has set aside an entire bay where you can walk your best friend.

Sophie, my ageing labrador, loves it, of course. A city dog, she is walked at least once a day, occasionally two or even three times. But I can understand that the regular round of pissed-upon

telephone poles, car tyres and dead possums grows stale with repetition. The legacy of her breeding calls. Labradors grew from a
line of sturdy water-fowling hounds and are seldom happier than
when they are wet. Being wet and chewing experimentally on a
captured bird is, for them, the first step on the path to nirvana.

As a pup, Sophie approximated this by leaping upon birds
drawn to our water sprinkler and enthusiastically shaking them
to actual pieces. As she has aged out of the killer demographic,
however, she has learned to find her pleasures elsewhere. The
beach is one such place—but not only because seagulls call forth
memories of blood and water.

She is not the hunter she once was and I am not naive. I know
only too well the reason our furry friend goes wild at the first
whisper of crashing surf is that she is already imagining the giddy
joy of befouling herself at water's edge. For this reason I normally
walk Sophie for an hour before we get to the beach. And I take
her at different times of day, lest she determine a pattern to
our outings and set herself the challenge of holding bowel and
bladder tight until some innocent child's carefully constructed
and much-loved sandcastle presents itself as a tempting target
for explosive discharge.

No. We walk and we walk the hot dusty backstreets until she
has done her dirty business and it is safe to have her off the leash
near sand and water.

Or so I thought, until yesterday. A full hour I gave her on
the lead, with multiple breaks to make potty and to water the
parched and yellow grass of Byron's less travelled byways. When
at last it seemed there could be nothing left, no chance of being
disgraced in public, we repaired to the surf.

A fine hot day it was, with a lovely rolling swell peeling
north of the small rocky outcrop that marked the edge of the
sanctioned area where dogs might play and frolic. Many children
were about, watched over by their parents, and many other dogs
too. All behaving and enjoying themselves.

I let slip the hound, who bolted after a border collie and took to racing back and forth up and down the beach, a pleasing sight after recent woes and injuries. We carefully chose the breeder from whom we took our pup. Frank Meusberger, a retired copper, was a thoughtful and conservative breeding master. He had never sought to produce the highly prized and hugely expensive brown labs you sometimes see. Force breeding that particular strain brings out the genetic hip problems that can torment older labradors.

Sophie, when young, was a small but sturdy animal, strong and fit. She maintained her fitness even as the years piled up on her, but had of late been bothered by arthritis. It was a pleasure, then, to see her move so freely and with such vigour on the sand.

Not that I allowed my normal vigilance to slip. I kept close watch lest she suddenly begin to display the telltale signs of a dog in search of a dumping spot.

But there was no warning. No telltale signs.

After running about for ten minutes with no sign of needing to take a canine comfort break, she suddenly charged into a small lagoon-like area in front of several families and, panting and smiling the way dogs do, let loose an enormous and distressing explosion of semi-liquid brown spray, carrying within it lumps of more solid matter.

It was as though time ceased to have meaning. A small bubble of suspended reality enclosed the beach. Waves no longer crashed. Gulls no longer soared. Other dogs stopped their charging about.

All was still.

And then one child, downstream of the toxic event, screamed.

Then *all* the children screamed, their parents yelled, and I roared at the dog to stop what she was doing. All of which naturally served only to reward her with the sort of attention that demanded even more panting and spraying and bounding about.

I was moving towards the contaminated site, slowly at first, in disbelief, but accelerating as the horror of it dawned. The children scattered, some hauled out of the sea by cursing parents who could not have splashed more had they been trying to save their charges from a great white.

Meanwhile, the dog, who seemed to have stored a week's worth of bodily wastes for this moment, continued to leap and spray and turn in circles. I had my phone in one hand, held high above my head, a doodoo bag in the other, and the eyes of everyone upon me as I raced towards the deposits, hoping somehow to scoop them up. Also racing towards them was an unusually large set of waves. Great fantails of water arced up behind me as I accelerated. Sophie barked in joy at such a jolly caper. Parents and surfers did not.

The waves made it there before I did, scattering and atomising everything while I traipsed forlornly back and forth making a pathetic show of launching myself at anything that looked even vaguely brown and collectible.

How long does one stay in the water and show willing under such circumstances?

For as long as anyone who witnessed your original disgrace remains.

We were a long time getting out of the shallows of shame.

Snake Dog

Anson Cameron

The old man called me into his office and told me we were
buying a horse. Something I could learn to ride on. He'd found
a mare in *Stock & Land* and rung the owner and arranged to go for
a test ride on the thing, he said. Come on, a lunchtime excursion.

Dad was wearing his aubergine business suit. He pulled on his
RMs and we got into his HD ute and drove out past the north
edge of town to the 10-acre hobby farms of Bathurst burr, car
bodies and lone sheep with Christian names.

We pulled up at a yellow brick veneer with a weed yard. The
horse was right alongside the house in a treeless paddock. A lean
chestnut mare. She looked sparky, alert. We whistled her up with
a handful of lucerne and I fed her through the fence as Dad got
the saddle from the ute. He cinched it tight and began to ride her
around the paddock.

I stood whacking the fence wires with a stick, Jimi Hendrix on a colossal five-string. I stopped when I saw the horse's owner peeking from behind his blinds, watching Dad kick her to a canter and test her flightiness by throwing his hand in front of her eyes. A lot of people were wary of talking to lawyers, broad daylight, face-to-face. They thought it might cost them—money or dignity, they knew not which—but somehow it would cost. So I understood why the guy didn't come outside. His horse was being ridden by a legal eagle in an aubergine suit. No need to get involved in that.

Dad rode the chestnut mare clockwise and counter-clockwise round her small paddock, taking her through all the gaits. She moved like she was auditioning for a life of wide spaces, hills, the bush, dawn journeys. He unsaddled her and I gave her an apple and we drove away with me wiping her slobber off my palm onto my bare thigh. He was impressed with the horse, though the owner was shifty. The horse was at least two years older than advertised. 'I could see the guy watching us from inside his house,' I said.

'Did he look shifty?' Dad asked.

'Furtive,' I said.

'Furtive.' Dad rolled the word round his mouth. The furtive are a favourite hors d'oeuvre of lawyers.

When we got back to his office, Dad phoned the owner and told him his horse was okay, she might do the trick, she was older than he'd said, of course, but she had a light mouth and wasn't skittish. 'How ... like ... how would you know that?' the guy asked.

'We came out just now and rode her,' Dad said. 'You must have been out.' He winked at me.

'Not my horse, you didn't,' the guy said. 'I been with my horse all day.'

Dad had got the wrong address and saddled up some stranger's horse. Had ridden some citizen's pet ... put the steed of some housebound innocent through its paces.

These years later I still see that guy peeking out from behind his blinds. What did he think we were? Joyriders? People who stole horses a quarter-hour at a time? How did he explain us to his missus? 'A guy in a purple suit saddled up Joybelle and rode her round the paddock today.'

'Bullshit.'

'True. Canter, trot, gallop, like … I don't know … maybe he's driving past and wondering how she rides, so he pulls over and he rides her to see if his speculations is on the money. Just curious.'

'And you didn't stop him?'

'I told you … he was wearing a purple suit.'

Next day we drove north again and Dad rode the advertised horse. It was thick-coated, thickset, and looked like it should be pulling a bucket, working underground. The sort of horse to make a prospective buyer umm and ahh and grimace. Given the umms and ahhs and grimaces, the woman there said she'd throw in a puppy. Her Australian terrier bitch had just had a litter of puppies. Terriers of tangled genealogy, Dad called them. Which she winced at, but he said was most Australian. He got me to choose one while he bought the horse. We gave the pup to my sister Vicki as a birthday present. She cooed over it, named it Bindi, bathed it once or twice, and then left home.

I never had a dog of my own. Legally bound to me—naming rights and feeding duties. Bindi was an absent sister's dog. She probably didn't know that, but she was. And a bitch. We didn't care for each other early on. Who, with any male dignity, with any plans to hunt mega-fauna and track Navajo, would want a puny, female dog as sidekick? She smelled my disapproval, but began to tag along on my expeditions when she learned there would be blood, speedy getaways, warm things falling from the sky.

We lived out of town on the Goulburn River, in snake country. The first serpent she engaged was a large eastern brown on our doorstep at night. Enough poison there to kill a congregation or a Samoan. By the time I answered her squeals they were joined.

I was to learn that if you could catch her in the early phase, while she was circling the serpent wailing, being drawn closer by the vortex of her bloodlust, you could snatch her up and stop the fight, save the snake ... or dog. But there's no way to unlock a snake and canine once they're fully involved. It's personal by then, and you'll be bitten by either or both for interfering. Bindi soon got a lock on it behind its head and shook it lifeless. And was thereafter hooked on battle. Tiger snakes, brown snakes, black snakes ... and one blue snake.

Wolves don't attack bears front on. Jackals don't latch onto lions. A cougar avoids a rattler. Snakes flee from all things. Nature is circumspect. You think a leopard swaggers and hums the 'Eroica' on its rounds? It proceeds like Stalin's proctologist— gently, gently, any slip death. Each wild beast throbs with the knowledge of its own fragility.

Not a terrier. They are impervious to prudence. We have bred prudence from a terrier's brain. The sensible were spayed. The peaceniks were neutered. We have crossed kamikazes with cra- zies and enticed the foolhardy to fornicate with the hotheaded. We have made a canine Scotsman. These small dogs are a type of homicidal lemming. One does not expect to see a country terrier with a trim of whitened fur around its muzzle. Geriatricism is as rare, to them, as honesty to a cat.

She was bred to play a charging Capulet to slithering Montagues, a snarling Hatfield to hissing McCoys. No other role and no chance of peace. A snake is a peaceable creature. It doesn't want to fight a dog. But she couldn't not. She was a duellist. Everything on the line every time. You only ever lose one duel.

She fought many snakes. The rebel yells calling up her courage, before the silence of battle. Each time, afterwards, Dad would scratch her neck and say, 'You won't make old bones.' He was saying it for me to hear.

One summer day I jumped onto the front seat of a car that had been years abandoned in the bush near our place. Alongside me was a massive tiger snake, curled, head raised, leaning back ready to punch forward. Its back was iridescent blue, sparking sun like a badass Harley. I was a skinny boy wearing footy shorts. Bindi came in through the driver's door across my lap. No circling, no overtures; blue chrome scales and black and tan fur and screech and hiss. I was out in the dry leaves swearing when that war finished.

She came to me and lay at my feet. Was she sedating as the adrenaline ebbed from her? Or being put out by neurotoxins? I was still on a combat high, my voice loud and my sentences full of 'fuck'. Fuck this and fuck that and Jesus Fucking Christ a tiger big as a fucking Harley. When I came down I lay beside her and scratched her belly. She was just tired. By now I realised that the snake that got her got us, so I told her, 'We won't make old bones.'

In the afterglow of adrenaline there was always a brief season of serenity. I came to expect it, to wait for it and relish it. A surprising fifteen minutes where we lay zonked in the dry leaves and stared at the sky, her tucked under my arm and the sun hot on us. Hideous Death had taken its shot and fallen short, and I felt dreamily immortal, as if all big battles would be won. Lying there I'd even feel a tinge of sorrow for the dead thing, and this sorrow was the sapphire set in the crown of survival. We pitied the fallen. There but for the grace of God … These were our closest moments. These little pools of serenity after the adrenal high of battle. We had waged soldierly campaigns and our cause was just.

I'd fallen in love with a thing that had a terminal addiction. Dad and I walked miles of bush calling her name, longingly, angrily, half-heartedly. You only ever lose one duel. She'd lost hers. I forked my fingers and whistled whistles as artful as prayer out through the box forest, hoping to reincarnate her. Knowing the whole time if she could come she would have come by now. Hack her kennel to kindling. Chuck her collar to the back of the outside cupboard among the junk. Hard to kill a missing dog, though. For long weeks the bush around our place held her live presence. And I whistled her when there was no one else around to hear.

Until, two summer months later while riding my bike, I glimpsed a swatch of jerked hide wearing telltale tufts of black and tan in the table drain by the wooden bridge over the Sevens Creek. I turned away so it never got to be more than that. A glimpse. A question. Not an answer. I told no one.

Because … because great warriors die in combat. Great beings wander off to an elephants' graveyard and sink slowly to the earth, their tasks fulfilled. They don't lie in ditches with their backs broken by Monaros. Bindi wasn't knocked over by a car. Bindi lies coiled in the infinitely ribbed helix skeleton of her enemy. Its throat is in her jaws, its fangs in her hide, and the fur-raising frisson of battle sings in her young bones.

The Horse Whisperer

Les Carlyon

Trackwork is ending at Caulfield. Carefully, for he is a methodical man, Robert Edward Hoysted picks up the badges of his trade: Thermos, flyspray, two ballpoints, clipboard, silver stopwatch, binoculars. In the distance, a farrier's hammer rings out its lilting song. The faithful are being called back to the stables.

In his sea-green jumper and old jeans, Hoysted strides off to groom his horse. His head is down, as though he's trying to figure something, and the summer breeze ruffles his grey hair. By choice, he's now a one-horse trainer, although he also helps Tony Vasil with his big string.

Seventy-one he is, and the number throws you because he looks and talks the way he always has. His hands are calloused, yet horses, an inordinate number of them champions, have always found their touch soft. With his pink cheeks and chapped lips, he looks like a farmer who has spent his life in the sun and the rain.

Suddenly, he snaps out of his trance. A group of youngsters has been watching trackwork from a stewards' tower. Now they clamber down the stairs, leaving the iron door of the box open.

'Boys,' Hoysted calls. 'Boys! Would you close the door, please. It frightens the horses when it flaps in the wind … thanks.' Then he says to a girl whose horse crow-hops at the sound of the slamming door: 'They're not horse people.' It's as though he's sorry for them.

The man is a perfectionist. Always has been. Every good horse he's trained has been treated as if it is the only horse in the world. His magnificent obsessions read like this: Scamanda, Rose of Kingston, Love a Show, Spirit of Kingston, River Rough, Sydeston.

And the big one. Manikato.

Now we go back sixteen years. It's Australia Day 1981, early morning and hot, too hot, 27 degrees already, a northerly teasing the dust. The right day for a bushfire, not a horse race. At his Mentone stables, the perfectionist has seldom been more nervous.

He's training this champion called Manikato—except now he isn't entirely sure what he's got behind the pink-and-blue door of stable No. 6. Oh, the red horse looks formidable, as a heavyweight champ should: big and thick, loaded up in the shoulder and with lots of bad disposition.

But something has gone wrong inside.

At his last start, ten months back at Randwick, Manikato bled and had a heart attack. Bagpipes frightened him in the mounting yard before the race. He played up badly. Briefly he looked as if he might barge into the jockeys' room. Maybe the heart attack started there, because as soon as the gates opened, Manikato tried to run out. He'd never done that before. Maybe he was swallowing blood then. No one will ever know.

They wrapped his head in cold towels and took him back to his stables at Rosehill. He bled all over the float. Soon, sundry experts, some of whom had even ridden on merry-go-rounds, said the horse would never come back. Mal Seccull, his owner, rejected a big offer from the United States, where bleeders are allowed to run on medication.

So here they were, on Australia Day, trying to win the William Reid Stakes at Moonee Valley for the third successive year, and more than a little trembly. As Hoysted said last week: 'It worried me that if he raced again, bled and dropped dead, you'd be castigated by all the people who loved the horse.'

And now the weather bureau was forecasting 42 degrees, better than 107 in real weather. 'I rang the vet when I realised it was going to be hot,' says Hoysted. 'He said the hotter it is, the greater the risk of bleeding—said something about the thinning of the blood.' Hoysted laughs. 'That made me feel better.'

For months, Hoysted had been testing Manikato for faults, looking for signs. And worrying. Extracts from his diary:

November 25, 1980: One-and-a-quarter miles, last four furlongs strongly—really well today. Weighed 1278 lbs [580 kgs approx.].

November 29: One-and-a-quarter miles quietly ... feels wonderful.

December 2: First gallop after bleeding attack ... last two furlongs in 27.25 ... pulled up clean in wind.

December 23: Last three in 36.25 easily ... no sign of stress.

January 6, 1981: Passed by Dr John Bourke.

January 8: Fastest work yet ... seems a much better horse.

> January 15: Sandown—4 in 50.5. Gary [Willetts, his race jockey] very pleased—me so-so ... blew a bit and seemed distressed—may be due to very hot weather.

> January 24: 3 in 34.75 ... brilliant work ... inspected thoroughly by vet. ECG, blood, etc, all well.

> January 25: looks to have tightened up nicely. Very hot.

Yes, very hot and getting hotter, and Manikato was famous for sweating.

How to stop him melting on the way to the races?

Another trainer rang with a tip: turn the two-horse float into a Coolgardie safe. The perfectionist loved it. 'We hung wet hessian bags on the stall divider. The wind hits the cold bag and comes off onto the horse.'

And the burly horse won his third William Reid easily, his neck wet with sweat, his hoofs throwing up puffs of dust. No pain. No blood.

The champ was back. The saga would go on. And on.

Extract from the diary entry for that day:

> Hosed he and Shilo [the stable pony and Manikato's best mate] before loading, put wet bags in trailer. Good at races considering heat ... Won ...

They're running the William Reid again today—except, in a small travesty, it's been renamed the Sunicrust Australia Stakes. Some flash horses are entered. But compared with Manikato, they're just handy.

Manikato would win the William Reid for five successive years, a feat comparable to Brown Jack's six wins in the Queen Alexandra Stakes at Ascot, England, and almost up there with Red Rum's three Grand Nationals at Aintree. Manikato is probably the best sprinter to have raced in Australia. And if he isn't up there with Carbine, Phar Lap and Tulloch, he managed one thing that they didn't. He was a champion for six seasons.

As a youngster, his stride was carefree. He'd come bounding around home turns with his ears pricked and win on sheer talent. As a seven year old, his stride had become ragged. Sometimes he'd try to hit the ground with both forelegs at once to spread the shocks over his worn legs.

Now he'd lay his ears back and grind home on courage. And on towels, plastic shopping bags, ice and bandages.

After Manikato had worked, Hoysted would wrap towels around his forelegs.

Ice was tipped into shopping bags. The bags, which assumed weird shapes, were bandaged onto the legs. A stranger coming upon the pair might have thought the horse had hopelessly crooked legs and that the grey-haired man kneeling in the straw was praying.

Hoysted first saw Manikato at the Adelaide yearling sales in 1977.

He didn't much like him. Seccull had Manikato's half-sister in training with Bob's older brother, Bon. Bon had told Bob to buy the colt 'if he didn't have any faults'.

'If he'd said: "Buy him if you like him," I wouldn't have,' Hoysted says.

What was wrong?

A pause. 'He just didn't look like an athlete.' Hoysted gives that shy laugh of his and looks down. 'He had a big boofhead and he was very heavy bodied.'

The experts, it seems, agreed with Hoysted. The colt who would be gelded and go on to win $1.1 million was knocked down for $3500, half of what Seccull, a Melbourne businessman, was prepared to pay.

Bon would train him to his 2-year-old triumphs, the Blue Diamond and the Golden Slipper. When Bon died in 1978,

Seccull gave Manikato to Bob, who would win another twenty-five races with him.

Chance had come into it too. 'If the sales had been two to three weeks later, Bon probably wouldn't have bought him,' Hoysted says. 'His half-sister became very hard to handle. She picked up a strapper in her mouth and threw him over the door of the box.' Manikato wasn't easy either. 'Even towards the end, we couldn't take him out for a walk in the afternoon. He'd just march you wherever he wanted to. When we were in Sydney, at Rosehill, I couldn't walk him from the stables to the course, even though it was only 200 yards away. I had to float him. There was nothing outrageous about him—he'd just march you about. He was so strong.'

What if he hadn't been so good?

'You'd have thrown him out of the place—too much trouble.' Strong words from Bob. He considers them, then—perhaps unwittingly—tells you one of his secrets.

'I think with great horses like him you've got to go along with them a bit and not break their spirit. You break that and you break what makes them great.'

When Manikato came in from the paddock on 18 December 1981, to prepare for his fourth William Reid, Hoysted had a new problem. The horse's legs had begun to go. At his last run, he'd pulled up sore and beaten.

Vets told Hoysted he was wasting his time. Manikato's offside suspensory ligament (the elasticised band of fibrous tissue that helps hold up the fetlock joint) had puffed up. From now on, he would race in bandages.

Extracts from Hoysted's diary:

December 24, 1981: Percy Sykes [the Sydney vet] not happy with leg prospect.

January 1, 1982: Leg not 100 per cent to look at.

January 12: Cantered from five furlongs, last two in 27.35. Action excellent … leg a bit blown later but better at night.

January 13: Good work at track. Seemed seedy—left feed. Temp. and leg up.

January 26: 4 in 52.5 … leg holding up fairly.

January 28: 4 in 48.14. Superb … leg excellent after ice treatment.

Manikato won the Reid easily, his legs a blur of white bandages. Hoysted had pulled off the nicest balancing act. He'd given the horse enough work to get him fit—but not so much that he hurt. He told everyone it was his biggest thrill in racing. He also told his diary. *William Rd. Travelled well, won well … My best effort.*

....

The Hojsteds emigrated from Denmark to Ireland. The Irish couldn't pronounce the 'j', so they became Hoysteds. About 1859, Frederick William Hoysted and his wife settled at Wangaratta. 'They had nine kids and were three months on the boat,' says Bob.

So you're a fourth-generation trainer?

'Fourth generation here, yes, but it could be sixteenth.' How?

'Well, one of our ancestors was the groom for Birdcatcher [the crack Irish racehorse of the 1830s].'

Bob is the son of Fred (1883–1967), who won seventeen Victorian trainers' premierships and turned out the champions Redditch, Rising Fast and True Course. 'Father', as Fred was known, took up jockeying at twelve.

Once, the Melbourne stewards called him in for failing to ride a horse out. He told them he would rather whack them with the whip than ride a tired horse. They gave him a month.

'My father was a very highly principled man—as I can be when I get my dander up,' says Bob. 'And he was terribly loyal. When Bon and I were kids working for him, we used to bet.' He laughs. 'We had to—there wasn't a lot of wages.

'Harold Badger was the stable jockey. He'd had a bad fall and wasn't riding too well. Which meant Bon and I were losing. We suggested to Father that Badger would have to go. Father took it very badly. "Harold Badger is my jockey," he said. "He will be my jockey as long as I want him to be. You boys be patient." Sure enough, Harold came good.'

Bob, too, inspires loyalty. When Manikato bled, the Americans offered Seccull about $250 000, a lot for a horse who might never race here again.

'In the end,' Seccull says, 'I said to Bob: "It's very tempting." He said: "He's your horse, it's up to you." To sell him, I thought, would be unfair to Bob, who loved him more than life itself.' When Bon died, Seccull received offers from big-time trainers wanting to take Manikato. He ignored them. 'I just liked the humanitarian aspect of Bob. I'll never forget when we won the Rothmans 100,000 in Brisbane the following year. We're all at restaurants and drinking up. Bob's gone to the greengrocer. Gone to get the horse a lettuce. "Manikato likes lettuces," he said to us.'

....

For his fifth win in the William Reid, Hoysted had to train a horse with two bad legs. Now the nearside suspensory was puffy, too. Extracts from the diary:

December 10, 1982: Came in from paddock. Looks a treat, legs fairly good.

December 19: Tendon swollen.

January 13, 1983: 600m in 36.9 … going really great but legs only fair.

January 14: Legs not good.

January 30: Stung by wasp, neck swollen.

Returning from trackwork on race morning—31 January—Hoysted wrote:

Really well, but legs do not look good. Very worried about him.

In the evening, he added this:

William Reid. Won beaut.

He did, too. It was the fastest of his five wins. And he had done it all on courage. Three starts later, in Sydney, Manikato ran his last race. He lost his action and turned his head towards the rail when leading in the home straight at Rosehill.

He returned for a sixth try at the William Reid, but the dream was doomed from the day the horse came in. 'I didn't like his hind legs,' says Hoysted. The horse had a mystery illness, nothing to do with his heart attack or wonky front legs. Because he was public property, everyone wanted to help. Hundreds of remedies arrived by post. Hoysted read them all—just in case. At one stage, he was driving to Cranbourne each morning to obtain milk from newly calved cows because it contained colostrum, a natural antibiotic.

Hoysted was sure—and he was probably right—the horse's immune system had failed. He tried painkillers and antibiotics. Pills and medicines were imported from the United States and Switzerland. Doctors from Melbourne's Mercy Hospital tried to help. Always the result was the same. Given a new drug, Manikato would improve—then go backwards. 'Sometimes, when I think about it, I could kick myself in the bum for keeping him alive that long,' says Hoysted. It's almost as if he's talking to himself.

'But ... but I kept hoping. In that eight-to-nine months he was sick, the longest I was away from him was seventeen hours. I went to Adelaide to pick up a horse, booked into a motel, ordered a steak while I had a shower, ate the steak, and drove straight home.'

In the second week of February 1984, the horse's eyes said he was dying. Ian McEwen, then Moonee Valley's chief executive, offered a gravesite behind the tote building. Hoysted went to box No. 6 about 5 a.m. on 13 February and found his horse 'in a bad way'. The skin had started to peel off his body. The decision was taken to put him down and take his body to Moonee Valley that evening.

'The vet gave him a dose of stuff and said he'd lie down and wouldn't feel a thing all day,' says Hoysted. 'At one o'clock he was up and running—or stumbling, really—around the box. We took him out to the sandroll and he went down.'

The vet came and put him down. It was painless, bloodless. Hoysted remembers one thing. 'It took a double dose to put him to sleep. The vet gave him what he thought was enough—and it wasn't.

'I'm concerned we never got to measure his heart. It would have been enormous. But that would have involved taking him to Werribee Veterinary Clinic, and they burn bodies afterwards and I didn't want him burnt.'

Manikato's body arrived at the Valley about 6 p.m. 'Bob's wife, Iris, came, too,' says McEwen. 'They were pretty upset. I took them up to the house and we had a few short ones.'

So here lies Manikato, grump, loner and world-beater. He lies under petunias of pink and white, his racing colours. Nearly always, there are flowers on the grave, little posies like those you see wilting in the heat of country cemeteries.

Hoysted sends flowers every 13 February. He used to send them through a florist. One year he went out and didn't like what had been delivered.

Now he takes his own.

And people who don't know what they're talking about will tell you the game has no heart.

Bird Brains

John Clarke

There's an old joke about a New Zealand farmer who turned up at the local hospital one night suffering badly from exposure. Once he'd been treated and was warm and comfortable, the doctors tried to piece together what had happened.

'I was just in my paddock,' said the farmer.

'Your condition was terrible,' they said. 'You were in a bad way. How long had you been there?'

The man thought for a moment and said, 'About three days.'

'But why do that?' they said. 'Your house is only a couple of hundred yards away.'

'I was trying to win the Nobel Prize,' said the farmer. 'I read about it in the paper. It's awarded annually to someone who is outstanding in his field.'

I was attempting to win the Nobel Prize at Phillip Island one afternoon last year when a large bird flew over the trees and swooped low over me and went up the paddock, gliding silently and effortlessly. It looked to me like a swamp harrier and in its claws was some small prey, about the size of a young rabbit. I was fumbling to get a camera out of my bag and work out what I was looking at, when a second raptor arrived and gave chase. They flew to the top of the paddock, both of them picking up speed until suddenly they were going straight up in the air, climbing almost vertically. There followed a World War II dogfight; very close encounters, tight turns, buzzing each other and veering away, changing angles and then soaring up again, and then, out of nowhere, the first bird, higher up now and apparently almost floating, dropped the prey in midair. The second bird turned and dived across the sky, gathering speed, and headed directly at the falling object, then grabbed it and took off, low and fast and deadly, back over the trees and away.

I had by this stage taken a number of inglorious and rather fuzzy photographs, and when I got home I sent them to a friend who is a natural scientist and who knows most of the birds in the area personally.

'Here are my questions,' I said. 'Are these swamp harriers? Is that a rabbit? And have I witnessed the hijacking of one bird's food, by another bird?'

'Yes,' said my learned friend. 'They're both swamp harriers. And yes, quite a good rabbit. And no. What you have witnessed is the following: in the breeding system the male swamp harrier is so fierce that he's not allowed into the nest in case he attacks his own young. So what you have witnessed is the transfer of food from the male swamp harrier to the female. They manoeuvre themselves into position in the air so that when he drops the food, she can fly onto it and grab it. She takes the food back to the nest to feed the young and he goes off on another mission, hunting for more.'

The fact that I had seen an elegant dance with strong evolutionary backing as a crude hijacking should have made me reconsider the way I looked at things. But my assumptions about the behaviour of birds continue to be almost completely wrong. I have heard birdsong coming from a tree and eliminated all the candidates one by one as they presented themselves, only to get home and find that the song came from the first bird I eliminated. The song was rich, operatic and deep and I couldn't believe it had come from such a small bird (a white-eared honeyeater). I have reasoned that a bird that cannot see or hear me will not fly away, and have been hugely surprised when another bird of the same species (Latham's snipe) spotted me and took off at alarming speed, beating up thirty or forty others and emitting an urgent squawking cry audible to every snipe in Victoria.

The other day I was changing a camera battery. This is the best idea I've had so far. I sat down near some bush and was getting myself organised when a little pink robin appeared not far from me and began feeding, darting from log to branch and tree to ground, working an area about the size of my office. Or, to put it another way, my office is about the size of a pink robin's office. A squadron of blue wrens bounced along, nipping insects off the ground and gossiping about what to do after lunch. A golden whistler was quietly busy in the trees above, picking food from the leaves and bark. And when I rather carefully got to my feet, I noticed that sitting on a big branch not far away was a white-bellied sea eagle. I had heard magpies and paid no attention. 'Magpies,' I thought. What I should have thought was 'The magpies seem greatly exercised by something. I wonder what it could be. Could it, for example, be an enormous sea eagle, which they are repeatedly bombing so it will clear off out of their territory?'

I had hoped that as I got older I'd get a bit smarter but I'm afraid there's no sign of it yet. Birds; that's where the brains are.

Man and Bird

Greg Combet

Every morning when I get out of bed there's a polite tap-tap at the kitchen window. It's a pair of cockatoos, waiting for breakfast. They're clever buggers—they wait until they see me, and after the first tap, I've got about thirty seconds to get their seed on the sill. If I'm too slow, they start banging their beaks on the window like hammers. When it's not the cockatoos, it's the rainbow lorikeets, screeching for seed and quite literally biting the hand that feeds them.

When I bought this flat, I had no idea it came with birds. I'd just retired from parliament after six years as a federal MP and minister. They were six of the most gruelling, exhausting years of my life. They were also the only six years that I didn't have birds in my life. I'd agonised over my decision to leave politics and everything that came with it—starting a new career from

scratch, moving back to Sydney, buying a flat in a part of the city
I barely knew.

The first morning the birds started lining up on my window
sill, it was like a sign that I'd done the right thing. I was home.
Out of politics and back among the birds.

People find my love for birds a bit odd. Tas Bull, a battle-
hardened, firebrand left-wing unionist who was my mentor in
the Waterside Workers Federation, once told me not to mention
my birds to the employers. He thought they might think I'm
soft, a pushover in negotiations. After a visit to my place to take
a look at the aviary, my birds won him over. Neither of us were
pushovers at the negotiating table.

A journalist for *The Bulletin* magazine who interviewed me
in 2007, just before I announced I was running for parliament,
asked me: 'Why do you like birds so much?'

According to the published story, I said irritably, 'Because they
don't ask questions!'

That's true, but it's not the main reason. More than anything
else, birds are a connection to my father—a living, breathing
memory.

When I was growing up on a winery at Minchinbury, near
Rooty Hill in western Sydney, birds were a big part of our life.
Well before I started kindergarten, Dad enlisted me as his helper
with the chickens. My chores included collecting the eggs to sell
to the Chinese family who had a market garden and fruit and
vegetable stall on the other side of the Great Western Highway.

After that, we bred pigeons to sell to a pet shop in Parramatta.
I enjoyed the car trip to Parramatta with Dad and the pigeons. It
was just the two of us, and I imagined I was contributing to the
family income in a small way. I did not, however, enjoy cleaning
up the astonishing amount of bird shit and feathers they used to
throw around.

Dad taught me how to handle rifles and shotguns at an early
age, and I revelled in it. Hundreds of starlings and Indian mynas

used to roost in the palm trees that lined the entrance to the property. In the evenings they made a hell of a racket.

The task was to keep these pests off the grapes at the nearby vineyard. They could seriously damage the harvest in each February's vintage, so I blasted them with enthusiasm. So did Dad. He nearly blasted me once, accidentally firing his shotgun in my direction, missing me narrowly. It was a shocking experience. Dad's father had accidentally shot and killed his own brother in a similar incident when they were teenagers.

But birds were not just for commerce or treated as pests. They were a pleasure my father and I cherished. We kept canaries for their song, and pheasants and peacocks for their beauty. We had many varieties of finches too. Finches were special, attracting greater care and attention and bringing greater satisfaction when they bred.

The finches had five-star accommodation. Behind the peach trees, we built a large aviary, with its own garden and finch habitat, in which we could walk around. It was large enough to house different varieties without causing turf wars. We had zebras and star finches, javas and double bars, cubans and longtails, and the beautiful Gouldians.

In those days Minchinbury was a rural property of several hundred acres owned by Penfolds Wines. My father tended vineyards and made champagne and table wines. He was immensely proud of his méthode champenoise Minchinbury champagne and sparkling burgundy. It irked him making sugar-sweet brands like Mardi Gras, designed for 'elderly ladies'.

Farm life forms bonds between people and animals. There was a milking cow and beef cattle on the property and, of course, my much loved dog. But it was the birds that took most of our time and attention.

Birds involved work outside, in the yards and the vineyard, and that was man's work. In the chook run and the pigeon coop I was expected to shovel dung, refill seed containers and refresh water troughs. If it wasn't done there'd be trouble, so I embraced the daily discipline.

My father died when I was thirteen. I was shattered. After that, bird keeping evolved into a sentimental pleasure, a pastime I still seemed to share with him, a touchstone of our relationship.

By that time I understood the breeding habits of numerous species. I was pretty good with peacocks: people would drive a long way to buy my young cocks and hens. But when we had to leave Minchinbury after Dad's death I had to trim myself to a suburban space and decided to focus on my favourites—finches.

Gouldians are a passion. They are endangered, so breeding them could help their survival. Their colouring is extraordinary: a bright red or dark black head ringed by a narrow bright blue band, green wings and purple on the breast and yellow underneath.

I have only one pair at the moment. Last summer, despite difficult breeding conditions, they produced two offspring that now fly hopefully to the door of the aviary each time I approach, looking for a spray of millet or some other treat. They seem to like me, don't ask for much, and never talk back.

Most people see birds and barely notice them. They'd be surprised to know how rich and complex a bird's life can be. In many ways, it follows the same extremes of experience as human existence: sex, death, fear, sorrow, joy, tragedy.

And sometimes it's a brutal world, just like our own. Coaxing my most recent Gouldians into breeding, for example, was a fraught process.

The cockbird put so much effort in, week after week, dancing, warbling, cajoling and building a nest, only for his efforts to go completely unnoticed and unrewarded. I was thrilled when the hen finally retreated into the nest that the cock had painstakingly built for her. In the privacy of the nest, a relationship consummated.

And one day, weeks later, the faint cheeping of babies. Four of them. I was as proud as any new father. Sadly, only two chicks survived.

A day after the fledglings emerged from the nest, one fell off the perch for no apparent reason. I found its body on the floor of the cage. A couple of weeks later a pair of butcherbirds attacked the aviary. One fledgling was literally frightened to death. The predators dismembered and ate the young finch, through the wire with their long beaks. A brutal world, indeed.

Through all the ups and downs of youth, the travails of union work and politics, and the joys and hazards of human relationships, finches and I have stuck together. There's been heartache at times: disease, cats, sometimes even unreliable children forgetting to top up the water when I've been on holidays.

Birds tend to shape the way people relate to me. Just about everyone gives me a birthday card with birds on the front. It's a well-intentioned default setting for family or friends.

Finches also lead to meeting other people. Just about the first people to welcome me when I announced my candidature for Labor in a Hunter Valley seat were the local finch fanciers. They'd heard about my finches from the media. Strangely enough, they were a bunch of guys about my age, from rural backgrounds, with Labor sympathies, and an involvement with finches since childhood. Completely normal, like me.

It was an immense pleasure to be welcomed by like-minded people. Pretty soon I became a subscriber to *Hunter Finch Fancier* and was invited to take the esteemed role of Patron of the Save the Gouldian Fund. Within my electorate on the western shores of Lake Macquarie was a massive Gouldian breeding and research facility dedicated to saving them. Hundreds of aviary-bred birds are transported to the Kimberleys and released in the wild, with regular monitoring and research to assess their progress and the survival of the species.

It's not all one-way. Finches have helped me, too. They were a calming influence during a working life punctuated by stress. During the waterfront dispute in 1998 I'd stand in the aviary muttering and swearing and none of the birds seemed to mind. I felt my birds supported me during the fight with James Hardie for asbestos compensation, and during the 'rights at work' campaign against John Howard's government I was convinced that the entire population of Gouldians, star finches, longtails, zebras and double bars were solidly behind the fight for workers' rights.

The demands of the parliamentary lifestyle interrupted my bird keeping for the only time in my life so far. I simply wasn't at home enough to look after birds. But as soon as I left parliament and moved back to Sydney, there were those cockatoos welcoming me back to civilisation. It was a sign. I set about building a new aviary for some Gouldians that I got, appropriately, from a bird dealer at Rooty Hill, near our old place.

Spending time with birds has soothed me during some of the most difficult periods of my life. And helped me feel close to my father and to my past.

That's what birds mean to me.

Acrocalypse Now
Trent Dalton

I assaulted the Cape York crocodile by the banks of the Wenlock River, remembering not to smile. I inserted the extended middle finger of my right hand deep into its cloaca, the fierce and ancient beast's slimy posterior orifice. I knew, instinctively, this was a first for the both of us. The tip of my finger found a small, fleshy organ along the wall of the cloaca tunnel and I gasped, sucked in the clean air of Queensland's prehistoric deep north.

'It's a boy!' I barked.

And everything changed. The scientists looked upon me with a new respect, a new kind of connectedness that can only come from digitally invading the private parts of an 8-foot apex predator.

'Well done,' said Professor Craig Franklin, a warm and soft-voiced University of Queensland zoologist, who, along with a thirty-strong team of scientists, animal wranglers, cooks and keen-eyed bushmen with unnervingly sharp knives, was deep into a ten-year study of crocodiles in the pristine river systems of the Steve Irwin Wildlife Reserve, a 135 000-hectare untouched Cape York sanctuary created by the Howard government in 2007 and run by the Irwin family as a living tribute to the late wildlife warrior.

I dragged my hand back out from beneath the crocodile's underside and raised a thumbs-up, my fingers dripping in cloaca slime.

Terri Irwin was lying atop the crocodile's closed and roped jaws, pride across her face.

'I think we'll name him Trent,' she said.

Some men have streets named after them, some men have libraries. I've got a killer crocodile swimming through the Wenlock, an archosaurian monster built some 200 million years ago as much for survival as for sparing every other creature on earth the burden of it. Trent's got a small satellite tracking unit fixed to his head, being one of more than 100 Wenlock crocodiles Professor Franklin and his team are tirelessly monitoring in the largest and longest croc study in the world.

It was Franklin's team that discovered crocodiles can stay underwater for seven hours. It was Franklin who tracked a crocodile as it made a groundbreaking and miraculous 900-kilometre overland odyssey to return, using its nose and evolutionary instincts, to its place of origin. Franklin wants to know where they've been and where they're going and why these great survivors have stuck around with us puny humans here on earth for so damn long.

The Wenlock River runs 322 kilometres to the Gulf of Carpentaria through an undiscovered country of savanna plains and dense wetlands and gallery rainforests filled with palm cockatoos and spotted cuscus and intrepid scientists from across the world who come to conduct studies on bird-eating tarantulas and rare ground lillies and collect samples for experiments in natural compounds to combat everything from cancer to malaria to TB. Boat upriver long enough, the Wenlock starts to resemble the river systems of Southeast Asia. Your whole outside-of-time-and-place-and-history boat journey goes all Martin Sheen voice-over, all *Apocalypse Now* surreal and endless odyssey.

And Ulysses was our Colonel Kurtz, our hulking 13-foot crocodilian Marlon Brando monster reptile waiting for us upriver.

'Ulysses,' whispered one seasoned crocodile wrangler, one of the brave souls given the ominous task of annually catching, releasing and re-catching the giant research crocodiles Professor Franklin tracks. 'He's pound for pound the toughest fighter I've ever caught.'

The smell of death drifted downriver from a bend in the Wenlock they called 'Chicane'. Franklin eased the throttle on the outboard motor of our tin research boat. 'That's about as close as you'll come to what a dead body smells like,' he said.

The smell was coming from a crocodile bait. Half a wild pig, what local bushmen called research 'volunteers'; a crocodile delicacy too rank and succulent for Ulysses to resist creeping unwittingly inside the weighted and roped net trap set on the muddy river bank, metres from the water.

Our team's four boats tied off against a tree a safe space from the trap. The air was hot and sticky. Clusters of flies like Kansas twisters buzzed around the pig bait. Inside the net trap, Ulysses was a huffing and puffing behemoth, a furious dragon who'd just lost his gold, dangerously rested. A team of eight scarred and leather-skinned crocodile wranglers delicately and laboriously wrapped a thick rope around Ulysses' jaws, using long poles like knitting needles to clamp his killer mouth shut.

'Puuuuuulllllll,' screamed the head wrangler, as eight men hauled Ulysses out of the trap, growling; a deep, guttural, prehistoric rumble from some place less biological than geological, some place deep within the earth, some place old and volcanic. The men needed to jump the crocodile to tape his deadly jaws but the setting was not ideal. The trap area was tight: too many trees for ropes to get caught in; too many roots to trip on. A mute tension filled the scene. 'His head's like concrete,' whispered Franklin. 'Don't go anywhere near the head. If he got a chance to swipe at you, he could snap your legs.' Crocodiles can whiplash, leveraging from the tail. Snap. And after snap invariably comes chomp.

Knees bent, hands out, Terri Irwin readied and braced herself to jump on the crocodile's head, some kind of crazy-brave warrior jungle woman-meets-devoted suburban mother of two.

'Terri will go first,' hollered the chief wrangler. 'And then the rest of the jump team, you will go like a stack of dominoes. Bang, bang, bang, bang. You've got to get in there and get those back legs off the ground so he can't push off.' The team lined up behind Irwin. Ulysses was furious. He began to death roll in the air, making great twisting leaps, arching, heaving, every muscle pulling the rope-wielding wranglers closer to his snapping jaws. Short, sharp directions were given.

'Too much rope. Coming round, coming round. Back, back, back.'

The ground thundered when Ulysses landed and then, to my eternal surprise, Terri Irwin leaped on top of the beast, the domino wranglers following behind her until nine or so people were stretched across mighty Ulysses' black and green back, pinning him to the ground so his jaws could be taped shut and so Franklin could swiftly and painlessly fix a satellite tracking unit to the back of the beast's head.

Her body weight still pushing down on the crocodile, Irwin nodded me closer: 'Put your hand on him.' I placed a gentle hand on Ulysses' head.

And that's when I saw my grandfather.

I don't know why he flashed into my mind at that precise moment but there he was, sitting in his armchair in the corner of the lounge room at the old house in Sandgate, not far from the lice-filled seawaters of Bramble Bay, northern Brisbane. The late Vic Dalton. Rat of Tobruk. Quietest, most humble grandfather who ever lived. Resting in his armchair, resting in peace, his war-brought wooden leg stretched out straight like a fallen karri tree, the great survivor, watching his tearaway young grandsons playing marbles on his lounge-room floor. A war hero, to be sure, my old man said. Even more of a hero back home, a bloke forever known in his sleepy Sandgate beachfront community as the dad who hobbled along the streets pushing his polio-suffering wife, Beryl, in a wheelchair; a bloke who hopped around on one leg in endless games of tag with his four kids on the Bramble Bay mudflats.

Ulysses, that great survivor, that dear old perfect killing machine, reminded me of Grandad.

It was something about his skin, so old and soft and journeyed. 'You're in the presence of a dinosaur,' whispered Terri Irwin. 'We still know so little about them. You get up close and they're soft and chubby like a baby's skin and then you learn that they're great mothers and fathers, extremely protective and intelligent parents.'

I leaned in close to hear Ulysses breathe, and the air from his nostrils lifted the hair on my forehead and it was clean and fresh like a Sandgate sea breeze. And, in that moment, I was sure I was close to some new insight into age and wisdom and existence; living and dying. There's a rare palm on the edge of the Wenlock River that takes sixty years to grow out of its surrounding tropical tree canopy and find the sun. It flowers briefly, only once in its life, and dies. In that moment next to mighty Ulysses, I was that palm having its first and fatal feel of the warm sun, briefly brushing up against some deep eternal knowledge, like there was something important to learn from Ulysses but my human brain was too small to understand what it was. Whatever that feeling was, it left as quickly as it came.

Mighty Ulysses was fitted with his tracking unit and, from a safe distance, the tape and ropes were carefully removed from his jaws and he slipped quickly back into his winding kingdom, the glorious and pure waters of the Wenlock.

We sailed back to camp and I sat at the front of the tin boat, eating from a packet of chilli beef jerky, trying to remember things about my grandfather.

I was humbled by the beast. I was saddened by him, too. He made me wish I had talked to my grandfather more. But you can't bring back time. Like holding water in your hand. James Joyce said that. *Ulysses*.

Masculine Shoes

Robert Drewe

Before leaving Los Angeles to hunt locations for Universal's new tropical island adventure–romance, Tyler Foss searched 'Queensland coast' online and came up with coral reefs, cyclones, crocodiles, ultraviolet radiation, partying high-schoolers, marine stingers and lost skindivers. He also found constant references to paradise on earth. Uncertain terrain, thought Tyler Foss.

As the advance guard, the person at the sharp end of any film project, the veteran Hollywood location scout paid close attention to his image: outlaw-rocker, with a lone-wolf air. He absorbed all the internet information about white Coral Sea sands, harsh sunlight, rainforest lagoons and salt-lashed boardwalks, gave his clothing the usual careful consideration, and decided, as always, on denim, leather and T-shirts. The only problematical item this time was footwear. Tyler Foss was fifty-five and 5 foot 7 inches, and at all times he wore custom-made cowboy boots.

After his thirty-five years in the business, the cowboy boots, along with the silver ponytail and chin stubble, the chunky Navajo bracelets and the unfiltered Camels, were part of the Foss persona—the Foss legend, he liked to think—set forever in the 1970s. They shouted wise-old-dog-knowingness and keeper-of-celebrity. And, incidentally, the heels added 2 inches to his height.

He owned two dozen pairs, including boots in ostrich skin (smooth and full-quill varieties), alligator (belly and back), snake (Burmese python and king cobra), lizard, caiman, conga eel, crocodile (Nile and Australian), stingray and kangaroo.

But on this assignment, much seashore reconnoitring over wet sand, cliffs and rocks would be required. Foss's bespoke boots averaged $4500 a pair. On the Massachusetts coast he'd lost his favourite king cobras while scouting *The Perfect Storm* for Warners. The cobra skin had quickly flaked and succumbed to the salty Atlantic fogs. Now, for coastal work, regrettably, cowboy boots were out.

An actual cowboy could not have felt more angst at giving them up. Eschewing the boots was a considerable blow to Foss's sense of self. He hadn't worn lace-up shoes, the footwear of the Suits, the Average-Joe citizenry, the office-going nine-to-fivers, since high school. But he was a professional, and intensive research into the best footwear for coastal tramping eventually turned up an alternative: something called the Nature-Grit sneaker. To Foss, the word 'sneaker' had a childish, suburban ring to it, not to mention the off-putting eco-hippie sound of 'Nature-Grit'. But it was made of yak leather, which sounded fairly exotic and hard-hitting, and came in suitably masculine shades: sand-yak, rust-yak, mineral-yak and—presumably for evening wear when traction was needed—black-yak.

Foss got a couple of pairs in sand- and mineral-yak. He was pleased to find they were surprisingly cool and comfortable on the job; moreover, that yak skin—perhaps it was the Himalayan high-altitude factor of the beast—really 'breathed' down here at sea level. After a long day's tramping through rainforest humidity or sand-dune heat, even without socks, they smelled less than regular sneakers. And, as he'd discovered on the Gold Coast, if you wished to undress quickly, especially after an evening's drinking, they required far less time and effort than boots. Cowboy-boot removal, Foss had to admit, could cost a man valuable impetus and energy these days, with sometimes depressing results. As well, the Nature-Grits were about $4000 cheaper than, say, his alligator bellies or conga eels. He could almost forgive them for the missing 2 inches.

For the whole late-autumn month of May—according to his research, a dry, benign, season-turning month in Australia, when anything cyclonic, venomous or man-eating should be absent or dormant—Foss roamed the north-eastern seaboard in his yak-leather sneakers, scouting the required adventurous-cum-romantic 'look' for the film, which was set on an unnamed tropical island in an unnamed ocean. And neither daytime saturation by sudden tidal surges nor night-time bar spillages and nightclub and casino scuffing could mar his Nature-Grits. Surf, salt, rocks and reefs, beer and bourbon drips, Camel ash: the yak leather resisted them all. Despite the effortless professionalism of his new shoes, however, even after three weeks' extensive searching, no coastal location seemed quite adventurously romantic enough in an original Tyler Foss way to recommend to the producers. He was becoming worried.

At an anxious ebb, Foss lugged his cameras and battered leather duffle bag (the sort that brought pirates or World War II air aces to mind) aboard a tourist ferry to an offshore island famous for its translucent sands. And as the boat slowly chugged along the scenic eastern shore, allowing the passengers their holiday snaps of migrating humpback whales, his anxiety began to fall away. How was it possible for a lagoon to be so clear, for a beach to be even whiter than the coral shores he'd just left? This sand was like crushed pearls.

What excited him as the boat drew closer, however, was the dramatic potential of the ornately rooted pandanus palms, lawyer vines and shadowy eucalypts poised on the edge of those pale sand-hills. The stark vegetation provided a sinister backdrop to the serenity of the shore. Winter storm tides had eaten into the dunes, and undermined trees lay toppled on the beach all along the high-water mark. Their exposed roots and claw-like branches now gestured at the sea and grabbed at the sky.

Lustrous sands, accessible jungle, crystal seas and menacing trees; Foss couldn't snap shots quick enough. He had a good feeling about this place: it should more than satisfy the director's and production designer's creative visions. The producer, too: the island was conveniently situated only thirty minutes from the mainland. Curiously, it did seem to be inhabited by many lean and tawny stray dogs, but as Foss and the other ferry passengers disembarked, the dogs skulked into the shadows of the wharf pylons and vanished into the rainforest. Easy enough for the animal wrangler to keep them out of frame, mused Foss absently, checking into his hotel.

His immediate task that first afternoon was to take some off-shore photographs of the island. Leaving the sand-yak sneakers on the beach, he rolled up his jeans and waded out into the shallows. For perhaps an hour, until the tide began to turn, he snapped away determinedly, capturing the main beach from many vantage points before wading back to shore. Strangely, he couldn't find his sneakers anywhere. They were gone. Stolen.

For a few minutes, Tyler Foss stamped the sand in fury and frustration. There was no one else around now. What sneaky son of a bitch would steal a man's shoes from the beach? Because he prided himself on travelling light, he'd packed only one other pair, the mineral-yaks. But, eventually, taking deep breaths, he told himself life would go on. He'd suffered worse tribulations than bare feet and stolen footwear—pneumonia, for example, while scouting sites for *Cold Mountain* in Romania (Romania had to pass for Virginia and North Carolina). Not to mention the king-cobra boot disintegration in Massachusetts.

As dusk began to fall, his temper finally settling, he padded back to the hotel with his first island location shots.

Showered and re-shod an hour later, his sanguinity returned, he sauntered out into the hotel gardens in order to have a customary end-of-the-working-day Camel and Jim Beam, to plan the next day's schedule, and to see what the night might bring. Seeing what the night might bring was Tyler Foss's favourite part of the day. Mostly the night brought nothing but a hangover, of course, but he was an evening-optimist by nature, unusual in someone thrice divorced.

Ever since he was sixteen, a short, pimpled boy showering before a movie date at the neighbourhood Rialto, this magic time of day had filled him with hopeful anticipation.

Anything could happen, especially in hotels; especially in hotels in foreign parts. As he well knew, when people were overseas, or on ships or islands, they did things they would not do at home. It was something to do with the sudden separation by water, the partition from their ordinary lives. And watching the last pink streaks of sunset fading between the coconut palms, and the deft fingers of the cocktail waitress adjusting a frangipani in her hair, he felt the old anticipative frisson.

As he sipped his drink, Foss became aware of some activity involving ladders and wires at the far end of the hotel gardens. A local film crew was bustling about and setting up under the palms. What was this? Already he felt a territorial imperative: this was his film location. He collared a passing gaffer and discovered they were shooting a beer commercial the next day. He tapped the loose shreds from a Camel, lit up, and through a spurt of smoke magnanimously informed the gaffer, 'I'm in the business myself.'

When the crew finished setting up, he invited them to join him for drinks. He was loudly convivial, as if he and they really were in the same industry, as if these Aussie TV-commercial makers and Universal Studios were even on the same planet. But they seemed amiable company, quite awed by him, in fact, and as far as he was concerned, any film crew in the world held more possibility of night-time action than a garden of tourists.

Meanwhile, the production assistants kept consulting clipboards and frowning at their watches, on the lookout for the commercial's director, producer and art director, and eventually there was a dramatic clattering in the darkening southern sky and from the direction of the Gold Coast came a helicopter. It hovered for a moment before landing by the swimming pool, discharging the people Foss's drinking companions were expecting, plus an attractive woman in a short banana-coloured skirt that accentuated her legs.

'That'll be her,' remarked one of the production assistants, with respect in her voice. 'That's the octopus stylist.' And it was. The octopus stylist had multihued bird's-nesty hair, a chirpy manner and a confident pointy chin reminiscent of the actress Reese Witherspoon. Tyler Foss was an old hand but he couldn't recall ever meeting an octopus stylist before, or even considering the possibility of their existence. From the moment of their meeting, however, when she generously joined the crew for drinks and ordered a mango daiquiri, he imagined that for the rest of his life whenever the subject of octopus styling came up, he would think of her.

Her name was Mia McKenzie. On the crew she was listed as 'cuisine art director' but her bailiwick was seafood and her forte was cephalopods. Octopus, squid, cuttlefish. Her job was styling them to look attractive on camera.

Apparently, she was in great demand for television, magazines and coffee-table food books. Her professional brief this time was to turn a smorgasbord of molluscs and crustaceans into an artistic display to sell more beer.

This TV commercial was intended to change the image of beer drinkers as sweaty, blue-collar pie-eating men with bulldozers and cattle dogs. (Those people drank lots of beer already.) The nation's middle-class women needed to be shown what a sophisticated and natural image a glass of beer could give them.

Hence the presence of six lean-waisted extras in a tropical island party setting, all wearing white, raffishly crumpled natural fibres while enjoying glasses of beer in the vicinity of tastefully designed fresh seafood. Hence Mia McKenzie's octopus styling. It had nothing to do with eating. It would be an exhibition, however fleeting its eventual moment on screen, to illustrate the sophisticated yet natural world of today's beer drinker.

All this Tyler Foss gathered as he competed with the crew for her attentions. For once his own range of impressive and scandalous Hollywood anecdotes was forgotten; he was tongue-tied by her rainbow hair, endless legs and vivacious manner. 'Lobsters are a cinch,' she was declaring. 'A spray of glycerine and they look fabulous. And crabs, too, once you've oiled them. Prawns, whole fish, oysters—any smelly old fish shop can style them. They're all a cliché.'

She was waving her arms for emphasis. Chopping the air. 'The shiny red lobster, symbolising passionate life, although actually boiled to death. The dramatic aggression of crab claws. The pink excess of a mound of prawns—just an invitation to gluttony. The oyster's sexual associations. Give me a break. Old, old hat. It's the octopus that stretches your imagination.'

'I can see how it would,' Foss said. 'All those legs. Or are they arms?' Oddly adolescent and awkward in her company, he gave a snorting laugh, which accidentally turned into a tobacco cough.

Her look was suddenly wary. 'Yes, there are those to consider,' she said.

'What about squid?' he asked. He couldn't believe he was labouring this conversation. 'There's no way a squid looks edible,' he stumbled on, self-consciously. 'Very ugly suckers.' His accent, thickened by bourbon and cigarettes, rumbled in the night air. 'I don't think I could style a squid,' he heard himself say. 'I guess I'd be more of a beef stylist.'

Mia McKenzie was staring at him now, squinting slightly, as if she normally wore glasses and wanted to really register his presence. The grey ponytail with its tinge of nicotine yellow, the elderly white stubble, the chunky turquoise and silver Navajo bracelets, the ageing-rocker garb. 'Yes, I've met a few homely squids,' she said, and turned her attention to the young assistant director on her other side.

Last drinks were called. 'Nightcaps in my room!' announced Tyler Foss, ever optimistic.

'We're shooting first thing,' someone said firmly, and within a few seconds the film crew had swept up the octopus stylist in their tide and surged out of the gardens. Alone, Foss stubbed out his final cigarette, sighed, stretched out his feet in their mineral-yak Nature-Grits. So much for comfort; without his cowboy boots he'd lost height and panache. He'd mislaid his humour and banter, and his successful way with women in foreign places. Wearily, he got up from the table.

Apart from some night creatures rustling in the bougainvillea, the distant throb of surf and the sudden hum of the pool filter, the hotel garden was silent.

Rising at dawn as always, Tyler Foss washed down some aspirin with orange juice and set out along the western shoreline to take more reconnaissance shots. The tide was out, a light fog blurred the horizon and his eyes watered in the sudden sharp sea air. A pale flurry of ghost crabs parted at his approaching steps, panicked back and forth, scattered into three groups, then re-formed and continued to bustle alongside him. For perhaps twenty minutes he strolled along the shore, occasionally snapping photographs, before he reached the eroded dunes and collapsed trees. This was what he was looking for.

This tortured beachscape would seal the deal. Already he could visualise the stark scenes on screen. And then he sensed he was being followed.

He turned quickly. There was nothing there. Only the dead fallen trees and twisted roots and the sheer sand-cliffs rising up behind them. The morning's only sound was the soft, wheezing rattle of the restless ghost crabs, like an asthmatic's breathing. He resumed walking. Again there was the feeling of being followed. Again he turned sharply. Nothing. He felt foolish and childish, like he was playing Grandmother's Footsteps or What's the Time, Mr Wolf?, reliving the suspense of those childhood games and feeling his heart beating faster. But this time he noticed prints in the damp sand, eerily close behind his own. Paw prints.

Tyler Foss stood completely still and eventually a thin, ochre-coloured dog emerged from a tangle of tree roots. Then an identical second dog. The dogs, both males, started silently circling him. He waved his arms and growled at them with all the throaty timbre of 200000 Camels. The dogs kept circling, as if judging their opportunities. Foss wished he had one of his shotguns with him.

The Browning 525. He recalled something from an African location foray and took off his T-shirt and stretched it above his head to make himself look bigger and more threatening. Apparently, it worked with leopards, animals unfamiliar with shirts, but the dogs didn't appear the least threatened. Soon another dog, a bitch, joined them. Foss threw stones and driftwood at them but the dogs took no notice, allowing his stones to bounce off their ribs as they slunk towards him on their bellies.

Then a flash of inspiration, born of survival, struck him. Fumbling with fear, thick-fingered, he undid one of his yak-skin sneakers and threw it to the dogs. Instantly, two of them fell on the shoe, fighting over it. The third dog kept coming for him. Foss tossed it the remaining sneaker—a mineral-yak, his last piece of footwear this side of the Pacific. He left them then, the dogs so busy tearing and devouring their yak meal that they ignored him.

Standing breathlessly at the counter of the general store an hour later, purchasing the only available footwear on the island, a discounted pair of pink rubber thongs, Tyler Foss learned that he had encountered dingoes.

He began the day's drinking far earlier than usual. Sheltering under a Cinzano umbrella in the hotel gardens, he was shrinking from all contact, human and animal. He was scared to leave the hotel grounds, much less to wander freely around the island. The dangerous-dingo problem; the footwear setback: he had much to consider. How could he recommend setting the film here, or indeed in Australia? Four weeks of scouting and nothing to show for it except the career-ending image of a cringing Halle Berry or a pale, shoeless Tom Cruise being bailed up by dingoes.

Under the palms, the beer-commercial shoot was under way. Foss was on his third bourbon, keeping his distance from the goings-on, when he spotted her bright hair bobbing and glimmering and was drawn by a sad mixture of desire, alcohol and curiosity to the smorgasbord being arranged by Mia McKenzie. That hair of many colours was hard to resist; she was the centre of attention as she prepared her display for filming. There was no doubting her status. Compared with her artistic endeavours with octopuses, squid and cuttlefish, the ministrations of the other food designers seemed insignificant, merely cheap craft. Even the usually superior ice carvers looked faintly ashamed of their melting dolphins.

Passing women—tourists and crew members alike—were shaking their heads in admiration as they spied the octopus stylist's presentation. Men, of course, hung in besotted fashion around her busy limbs and parrot hair.

Wielding cans of canola oil, glycerine and hairspray, her fingers a blur of motion, dabbing here and there with pastry brushes, spraying and anointing and smearing, rearranging errant tentacles and erecting complex cephalopod structures with hidden toothpicks, she was sculptor, engineer, architect and painter.

'Your feet!' she yelled suddenly. 'Love your feet!'

She'd spotted him. Tyler Foss flinched, waved an embarrassed hand and on his $3.50 ladies' thongs began to flip-flop back to his sheltering umbrella.

'See you at the wrap party tonight!' she called out.

So, of course he turned up at the party. And inevitably the octopus stylist was being swamped with male attention. All evening she was trailed by some infatuated actor, electrician or assistant producer. But she handled every overture as deftly as she'd managed the day's suckers and tentacles. At 2 a.m. her laughter still trilled from the hot tub. Beside her in the warm bubbles reclined Tyler Foss. Mia McKenzie put down her daiquiri, laid a hand on his arm, and eased closer. Tonight the distant party buzz and the surge and gush of the hot tub drowned out the pulsing of the surf. The gardens were quiet. Even the four dingoes bolting down the seafood display under the palms made no sound.

'You make me laugh,' she was saying to him. 'The pink thongs, fracturing your image, turning it on its head. I love that.' One thing Tyler Foss was good at was reading the signs. So he went with the flow of the evening and kept the outlaw-rocker dude more or less under control.

Next morning the helicopter came for her ridiculously early. But, as she said to him, there was no time to waste. There was calamari to be arranged in Noosa.

Cat and Moustache
John Elder

1.

A beautiful cat with a strange moustache lived in the place above the river where people came to die. The little cat wasn't there to say whose time was coming any moment now. I followed her from room to room, thinking this was her purpose. But she didn't climb onto the beds and stare knowingly into the fading light; she wasn't one of those chink-eyed slinkers-in soaking up the last of the warmth from bird-empty bones. And there was nothing to suggest that this small, beautiful painted-faced cat witnessed the freshly hatched souls leaving their bodies, as folklore might have it. I had read stories and seen unpersuasive photographs of such death-kin cats, what might be called spirit guides in the language of the caftan, but she wasn't one of them. She was spookier than all that. Her movements weren't slinky or fat-boy plodding but like something spilt, bled from the night itself, shadow-tiding. When a couple of people died in the blue-light hours, she seemed intent on herding me (in the manner of spreading water) away from the scene, to keep me engaged in our new friendship, leading me to something new on that very cold night more than twenty years ago. I had gone to the hospice on the river on assignment, to talk to the nurses and the dying residents, to watch a long night go by, to write up the intimate rhythms of gentle carriage and fitful surrender. It was a beautiful place in its own sobering way, an enlivening place to be, many beautiful moments with people long gone. The little cat is now dead too, and yet, in the fanciful elevating way of memory, she returns to my side now, my first companion, the one who introduced me to birdwatching in the dark.

....

2.

I have a friend who talks bitterly of putting aspirin into saucers of milk. He talks this way when visiting friends who happen to keep a cat or two. We all laugh off his murderous gripe, yet know him to be sincere. He's confessed to throwing possums off cliff-tops because possums aren't native to his homeland. He's all for the natives. I am yet to decide if there is cruelty in his glee, or is it self-righteousness buttering his heart? Like me, this friend of mine has a deep interest in and, yes, love of birds while knowing the birds themselves aren't burdened with (what we think of as) love in their attachments. He, too, my friend, admires the cat as a killing machine. He's not above paying tribute while just as quickly turning the talk to felinicide: o let him count the ways. But where he will throw a rock or a shoe and, on one occasion, a grapefruit at some cat hunkered in the grass, citing the vulnerability of wrens flitting in the shrubs or the spotted turtle doves bobbing brainlessly in the driveway, I'm more inclined to sit and watch and ponder how a cat makes its choices, how and when it gets turned on to tear-apart possibility. Why does it leave those wrens and turtle doves unmolested for half the day before turning on them like a sprung trap? Or, ignoring the quarry close at hand, why does it suddenly raise its head because of some subtle movement in the trees, desperately alive to what's perching there? What is it that brings a cat into its full primal killing self?

....

3.

There was a wire cage hanging from the ceiling, three or four little birds—canaries, I suppose, I can't remember. The lighting, too, I'm not sure of. Recessed or a flat-faced globe on a bracket high in the corner. I do recall thinking it couldn't be comfortable because the beam of light, no matter that it was dimmed, came down directly through the cage, throwing a soft shadow, low on the opposite wall. That's where I first saw her, sitting among the shapes of bird and wire cage, unmoved by the sprocketing chirpers.

I walked across to meet her: small black body, white socks and face, and that strange black moustache growing separate to her whiskers along the top of her pretty mouth. Cats either say hullo or they don't and she didn't. She looked at my dangling hand for a while and turned tail, walking into a corridor where a plaster saint with the face of a baby watched her in passing, a cold, gentle eye on the little cat's wandering through the very soft light. Some of the many renderings of Jesus on the long, pale walls looked down upon her, too, from pictures where they walked in light or hung from their crosses.

I followed along and watched her stop at an open door. Together we looked through the doorway at a man sleeping flat on a stretcher next to his wife, who was in a bed, slightly propped. These people were in their seventies. The woman didn't want to be alone at night. The man went home in the mornings to shower and eat something, water the garden, then back by noon to feed his wife lunch. That day he'd gone home to mow the lawn. On the way back to his wife he'd become confused in the traffic and missed feeding her lunch but he stayed to feed her dinner in the early evening. Soon after the dinner I'd bumped into him in the cafe lounge area. That's when he told me the story about mowing the lawn and so on. And here he was now, no talking: his wife asleep and it looked like he was sleeping, too. The cat sat in the doorway looking at them, with the authority of someone in uniform. She walked in and rubbed herself against the stretcher in two long passes. A little later we walked by their room and heard the wife waking and the man saying it was all right. I followed the cat leading me up and down the corridors, through the lounge area and back again, now and then standing at a doorway, so many doors open to the very soft light and so many forms of Jesus on the walls, despairing and at peace.

A couple of hours went by this way until we reached a door that led outside. She bumped it with her head. There was a heroin crisis at the time and the nurses liked to keep all the doors locked but the cat, bumping her head and waiting, demanded we go out. It was cold enough to make your fingers burn. Cold mist in the trees but clear in the sky, cold moon. I squatted down and she stood next to me, staring into the darkness of the trees, raising her head and opening her chest up, as a lion does to the sun. Then came that ghostly golden light, where the eyes become disks floating in the sockets, lit up as you find in a cheap battery-powered toy from a Chinese store.

I almost asked what was happening.

As she fluffed up all over, a cry came from the trees, a cat-like cry, but bird-like too, full of hurt. What I knew to be the owlet nightjar, the smallest of the night birds, with the dopey-kitten eyes, the baby-bulb eyes that don't reflect light; no matter if we had gone into the trees with a torch, there'd be no spooky red light, just startlement. There'd be no seeing them at all, most likely; they tend to hunt in pairs. Despite the chill I felt a rush of warmth. The owlet nightjar, rarely seen but much wondered at: in photographs the plump body doesn't appear capable of intricate blind aerobatics, no obvious jet fighter. From recordings I'd heard that squeezed-out mewl and now, in close company with the turned-on cat and its hammering heart, here it was. I'd read that in olden times, in olden countries, the nightjars were said to suck the blood from cattle, when in fact they were hunting the insects that swarmed the stinky beasts. Take a walk on a golf course, welcome swallows will do the same thing around your knees. Welcome swallows can almost be summoned if you know where to walk; the owlet nightjar makes itself known by surprise, almost never to be seen, only heard. I wanted more. Cat and man waited for more, but three cries only and the cold seeping in. We headed back inside.

....

4.

It's a pleasant thing to do, walking up to the local parkland with a pair of binoculars, searching out the parrots and finches and thornbills, the butcherbird high up with its eyes a bulging, hungry obscenity. It's like hunting Easter eggs. Aside from surveys done for my ornithology studies, I've not taken birdwatching seriously, not on dry land anyway. Where I crave to be is on the rear deck of a boat on the Southern Ocean, being tossed about and bitten by the wind, face-to-face with an albatross or a petrel, almost close enough to touch, quiet and unblinking. I'll be out there at four in the morning, not caring if my ears snap off, dead to every care I've left mouldering at home. Let it storm. If I were to be dying, this is where I'd want to be. Failing that,

I'd love to hear the owlet nightjar one more time. I keep trying. And where the little cat led me to the bird of the night, the bird, the desire for the bird, has led to a mission that I serve from time to time.

············

5.

In a purpose-built heaven for children, one might include a vending machine for hot chocolate that automatically puts three teaspoons of sugar in the bottom of the cup. Such a machine exists; not in heaven, but close enough. It stands in a bright, loud area off the entrance hall of that same hospice I first visited twenty years ago, where the rooms are quiet and dimly lit and so too the corridors, but this L-shaped area is loud with motors blowing in clean air and dragging out the bad. There are fridges for food and an ice machine and under the sink an urn hums with water on the boil. There are some tables and chairs arranged in cafe formation, lit with unforgiveness as one finds in a 7/Eleven store at midnight. Some books and games and magazines are piled neatly on shelves in the corner near the coffee machine. One of the books has 881 pages. It is hard to imagine dedicating one's last days to all those pages. Although doing so might speak of defiance: 'I'm not dead yet.'

Here she comes, saying as much, a woman not a child, but her straw-coloured hair is that of a young girl getting ready for a party, tied in a loose bun that hangs wantonly off the side of her head. Her pyjama pants are of a silky ballooning cut, wildly patterned. She has a child's arms and what might be taken as a shy craning of the neck, which is in fact a distorting of her bones. The biggest thing about this woman is her voice but I haven't heard it yet. It's hard to know how old she is.

What I see first are the wheels of her walker coming around a corner and stopping at a glass-doored fridge, which she very slowly opens and inside which she thoughtfully places an unopened cup-sized container of orange juice and an uneaten sandwich. She closes the door and looks at the sandwich as if it is a museum display. She moves forward to the ice machine and I see now the yellowing of her skin and the swelling and drooping of her lips. She pulls on a plastic blue glove and scoops ice into a plastic jug set on the seat of the walker. She turns away and heads out of view and I think that's that until the wheels appear once more. I am sitting at a table near the vending machine. My digital tape recorder is running. It is getting on to midnight, a Saturday night, 1 September, the first day of spring after a long and silver-sky winter. It has been a lovely clear day with the biggest blue sky that Melbourne has seen for some time. The night has gone cold again and I imagine so many people shuffling into their kitchens for a last hot chocolate before they go to bed. Here she comes now, with a blue mug in hand, walking solo to the vending machine. My briefcase is in her path.

'You're right,' she says, when I make a fuss.

'I see they've got it set up to have three sugars.'

'I know. Isn't that shocking? I only have the one sugar.'

'Right.'

'So it's a bit fiddly.'

She sets the cup in the machine and presses a button and stands and waits with her back to me. And then she says: 'Sometimes it's out of order. For three or four days.'

'Is that right?'

'If you look in the kitchen, you'll see all the mugs are gone.'

'Can I help you with anything?'

'No, no.'

She doesn't put her eyes upon me but says a shrike's good night and starts to turn away. I have an MP3 player hooked up to a little speaker and I press play. The urgent piping of a grey butcherbird comes forth and she smiles with surprise. She smiles by bringing her drooping lips together.

I'm smiling with my new nameless friend, explaining that the butcherbird lives in a tree, in my street, just across from my apartment building. As I'm talking, I'm noting with some relief how she is drawing closer and now I'm on my feet, pulling out a chair.

'I have about twenty different bird calls on this thing,' I say.

'What are you doing with them here?'

A couple of tubes dangle from the short sleeves of this small woman's T-shirt. She has unplugged herself from drugs and saline. She now sips from her mug of hot chocolate as I begin to tell the story of the little cat and the joys of birdwatching in the dark. I don't get very far. Something is hurting her.

'I need to go to bed,' she says, but she hurts too much to stand. I go in search of a nurse. Others get involved. I think of a broken horse I once saw at a rodeo being surrounded and escorted out by so many grim-faced men.

An hour goes by, sitting by the vending machine, waiting for someone new to talk to. No luck. I head outside and sit on the porch, where the smokers come, but none do. I try once more for the owlet nightjar, sending its recorded call into the trees. No luck there either. I'm still sitting out there at three in the morning when my nameless friend, the woman with the craning neck, finds me.

'I'm too wide awake,' she says, then tells me that her boyfriend and father are asleep in the chapel. I ask her: 'Would you like to say hello to a scarlet robin?'

She doesn't think there are robins in Australia. 'I thought they were English,' she says and I tell her about robins in folklore being friends of Jesus. One was said to have plucked a thorn from his head. Others were said to have wiped the tears from his eyes with their wings. There is also the story that robins are blessed because they keep company with the newly dead, and they won't abandon them until the bodies are committed to the earth. It's a good story, but awkward and intimate in this place. Instead

I press play and six breathy whistles travel into the trees. It's the whistling sound a child makes or perhaps a person missing half their teeth. I feel a very cold hand on my arm. Six little pensive whistles have returned to us from the dark, out of the trees. Her cold fingers are tapping my arm. And I look into a face I haven't seen before.

Rein Lover

Jonathan Green

The rain is hard, cold and near horizontal. We're riding straight into it, flat chat at a fast canter drumming insistently at the verge of a gallop. We spread over the high-country snow plain, breaking with a leap from a low, scrubby tangle of winter white gum and lifting the pace. The horses—fit, certain, little mountain types—toss their heads at the chance to stretch their legs, hitting out in suddenly open country. We lean forward out of the saddle, poised on the balls of our feet, flexing to the swoop of the horse, hands low and tight on the withers and moving to the regular, reaching rhythm. Fingers are numb with cold and tangled with soggy strands of flying mane, the coat flaps behind, mud and clods fly from the steely flash of hooves.

The ground is flat, running on in a long, sweeping curve 200 metres broad between two enclosing kerbs of snow gum. Flat, open country, but still a precarious mystery. Whatever rocks, logs, streams or dips there may be are hidden until the last moment by tussocks of calf-high alpine grass. From the middle distance, you get the impression of a long, uninterrupted meadow. It's not, maybe, but that's the fun of it: the uncertain plunge at wind-rush speed, eyes blinded by rain, charging into a great throttling hand of cold air with the constant shadowing possibility of an instant neck-snapping death. Or at least a bloody and bone-breaking stumble, a quick, irretrievable chaos of legs and hot, heavy careening flesh diving, rolling, tumbling to the ground.

We pull up at the far edge of the plain, horses and riders breathing hard, walking off the run. And then you stand and sit, wind and rain suddenly stilled, and drink in the slow-gathering mauve mist of early evening, the horse snorting plumes of steam that mix with the cry of birds shrieking for dusk as you amble towards the tree line and camp. And it fills your heart.

But not for the horse, who simply moves on to the next entirely captivating moment with slow, gentle grace, a moment sufficient to occupy its entire slim intellect, a moment linked to a lifetime of others by a thick stream of undilutable but simple memory of what brought comfort and what brought fear. And what brought food. Now the job of riding's done, he won't want to curl up with you like a dog or yap at your heels. He has no mind for it, no need of you. He'll just want to eat and quietly go, passing the evening happy in the familiar, secure comfort of the herd, chewing whatever it is in the herbivore world that passes for the fat. The horse will not romanticise the setting, the sense or the situation. It can't. No mind for that either.

And there it is, the nub of this complex, compelling thing between horses and the people who ride and admire them: a vast gulf in the perception of experience.

The horse had modest beginnings. Hyracotherium first appeared 50 million years ago, a timid leaf-eating mammal the size of a beagle, picking its way through the boggy, humid forests of north-western America and Europe on multi-toed feet. This was the Eocene period. From here the line that would one day bring us Phar Lap, Black Beauty and *Mister Ed* would go through a series of evolutionary conjugations, from mesohippus in the Oligocene, to merychippus and pliohippus in the late Miocene. Finally, 2 million years ago in the Pleistocene, came equus, a creature that combined four toes into a single, fleeter, hoof and adapted its teeth to the slow spread of grassland. It was faster, taller, recognisable to the modern eye and had the run of plains across Asia, Europe, the Americas and Africa.

It would not interact with man until it appeared on the menus of European Cro-Magnons some 50 000 years ago. Which was the beginning of a sometimes strange, sometimes cruel, some-times wonderful association, one that would, through fortuitous twists of long-forgotten circumstance, put man on a horse's back somewhere on the Ukrainian steppe at about 4000 BC. From there on, the evolution of the horse, its breeding for strength, speed, endurance or beauty, would be dominated less by the dictates of the wild and more by human need and desire.

They might have been out there somewhere in the service of humans for six millennia, but I never met one face-to-face until my late twenties. It was a winter Sunday in a Gippsland stable fragrant with grass and gum, the first sniffs of wattle and a thick fug of horse. About twenty of them poked out from their stalls, breasting the confining chains, casting a curious sideways glance and a half-dilated nostril at the intruder, calculating his level of threat at somewhere close enough to zero and resuming breakfast.

They were instantly captivating. Big. Warm. Breathy. Strange. Slightly dangerous and, to the novice, utterly unpredictable. Doe-eyed and gentle but with an undercurrent of the white-eyed and wild. Strong but graceful. From here I entered a slowly unfolding mystery, one filled with the quiet tension that naturally falls between a tentative human initiate and a tense quadruped whose primary instincts are fuelled by fear and a consequent desire for flight. The riding was awkward—and still can be, twenty years on—but it was the first canter that put the hook in, breaking from the jaunty one-two impossibility of the trot into a gently rocking three-beat—wow!—that had us coasting smoothly up a slight incline, me bouncing hideously in the saddle as the placidly suffering trail horse shuffled through his paces according to well-worn routine.

To ride a horse well is to interact with another species in a remarkably sophisticated way, one that requires the opening of communications between two minds and sets of instincts that run in awkward and unfamiliar parallel. It's an enduring, unresolved enigma.

Enthralled by it, I had lessons and bought strange clothes: moleskins, jodhpurs, oilskins, boots and an utterly unconvincing rabbit-felt Akubra. I'd been inner urban, rock'n'roll, late nights and cigarettes, and slowly I was turning into Adam Lindsay Gordon.

> Dark-brown with tan muzzle, just stripped for the tussle,
>
> Stood Iseult, arching her neck to the curb,
>
> A lean head and fiery, strong quarters and wiry,
>
> A loin rather light, but a shoulder superb.

And, like Gordon, there came a day when I took it all a step too far, a day when, overwhelmed by a vision of equine grace and beauty, I committed the rashest act possible in the thoroughbred dispersal saleyard and bought one. The first of many. A wild-eyed, hyped-up reject from the same line as Rain Lover but with a fraction of the racing talent. It ended in tears, the first, again, of many.

But that's the thing about Australia, there's no shortage of horses ready to be squandered on the ill-informed and over-ambitious, and by international standards they're going cheap.

They arrived on the First Fleet, two stallions and five mares that were part of an extraordinary complement that also included kittens, puppies, five rabbits, thirty-five geese, eighteen turkeys, eighty-seven chickens, 40 tons of tallow, 747 000 nails and 589 women's petticoats.

What became of the petticoats is lost to history, but by the turn of the nineteenth century there were 203 horses in the colony, and an uncounted number of strays. These soon had a name, a first sign of purely local equine lore. Private James Brumby, of the New South Wales Regiment, was a landholder from 1794. He ran horses, many of which he left behind when he moved on to pursue fortune in Van Diemen's Land. 'Whose horses are they?' colonists are said to have asked. The answer had an enduring ring: 'Brumby's.'

By the turn of the twentieth century there were 1 620 420 horses, more or less, in the new federation. In recent years we have become less particular in the counting. Estimates of Australia's contemporary horse population swing between 900 000 and 1.8 million, all of which—other than 300 000 or so freewheeling ferals—are engaged in some sort of relationship with humans. About 31 000 thoroughbreds are in training for various feats of athleticism. Others go to pony club—8000 or so in Victoria—work the farm, compete at dressage, show-jumping or eventing, keep law and order, hunt, play polo, ferry tourists in slow circles of various CBDs or simply hang out as pets. They are thoroughbreds, standardbreds, Welsh mountain ponies, Appaloosas, palominos, Andalusians, Irish sport horses, Connemaras, Shetlands, Percherons, Criollos, half-Hungarians, Australian stock horses, Arabs, Clydesdales, Hanoverians, barbs, Trakehners and don't knows.

We treasure—even dote on—their wildness, but we've all but bred it out of them, creating an animal that still runs on deep instinct but one that has been engineered over generations to suit our tastes and needs. The resulting bloodlines are narrow, worthy of a royal family. All thoroughbreds, for example, descend from just three eighteenth-century sires: the Byerley Turk, the Darley Arabian and the Godolphin Barb. Every other breed is as profoundly incestuous.

As a result, we have produced a rare population of beasts, animals docile, domesticated and seemingly wilful and untamed. Intellectually unfathomable in some ways, yet capable of extraordinary feats of memory and learning. Able to lash out in confused annoyance, to rear and run away, yet still bend to the arcane subtleties of the dressage arena, or the everyday acquiescence of allowing a saddle, a bridle, a ride.

This is the raw energy we harness when the horse performs, the wild, thoughtless impulse that can also have us pitching, in the instant of a buck or shy, to the ground. It is a tension between the learned and the instinctive that can never be quite resolved, an issue between humans and the horse that can only find its end in mutual trust.

At the Victorian racing industry's Hall of Fame there is one sight among the rooms of memorabilia, paraphernalia and time-hardened tack that comes close to an illuminating equine revelation. It is the skeleton of Australian racing legend Carbine, a set of bones not all that different from any other thoroughbred's. The legs are long and fine, the neck arches out in powerful vertebrae the size of bread plates. At the quarters there is a sense of the enveloping mass of muscle and ligament that propels two-thirds of a fleshy tonne at better than 60 kilometres an hour. And there's the great barrel of ribs, home to a 5- or 6-kilogram heart and lungs big enough to shift 150 litres of air a minute at the walk and 1800 at the gallop.

Which takes us to the head. Big, empty sockets for eyes that are the largest of any land mammal. The ears are just as sharp, capable of hearing at sensitivities above and below the human range. This is a machine designed to do little more than apprehend danger and flee from it at speed.

Somewhere here, too, hard to see, is the tiny cavity that houses the horse's brain, an organ of no great size or sophistication, one that even lacks the physical attributes that in other species enable imagination, insight, introspection. Or love. It makes a mockery of all the anthropomorphic baggage thrown at this simple creature. It has no will to be 'broken in'. It could hardly have courage or desire, least of all be thrilled by a race-day crowd roaring its name. It has memory, hunger and a sense of comfort and certainty. For as much as Jungians might single it out as a dream symbol of the higher, inner self, the horse is not a human being. A horse, as *Mister Ed* once so nimbly put it, is a horse. Of course, of course.

But no less put upon for all of that. Since 1345 BC and Kikkuli, horse master to Suppiluliuma, the Hittite king, we've had theories of horsemanship and equitation, theories that have ultimately rested on the horse's remarkable capacity to submit, through an intricate physical language based on balance, pressure and release, to the demands of its rider. This is the paradox of a beast we idolise as wild, muscular and wilful, but one we insist should turn a balletic piaffe for the sake of Olympic dressage glory if we ask it long and often enough.

The horse in work places its wellbeing almost entirely in the hands of its rider. The lowered head of the horse moving forward on the bit is a perfect example of this utter submission. The horse in this attitude is accepting the presence of the bit in its mouth and—in dressage, for example—will perform the most intricate choreography while barely fluttering a nostril. But the horse in this position is also almost utterly blind to anything ahead of it.

The horse's eyes provide almost complete 180-degree peripheral coverage, but they also have an inbuilt blind spot to the front. A horse approaching a jump in showjumping will not be able to see that jump for its last stride and will leap out of memory and faith. The horse moving liquidly nose down in dressage can see nothing ahead other than the surface of the arena directly under its nose. It places itself utterly in the hands of the rider, this from an animal whose first instincts are to constantly assess the world for threat and flee from it at an instant. We've bred them for supine docility. Trained them all their lives to give so readily.

Simultaneously we've made much of their raw power. On the elevated mound behind Melbourne's floral clock is an imposing statue of Edward VII. The king is mounted, as befits his station, and gazes out from the saddle with an air of calm disdain.

The horse? The horse is beside himself. The head is over-bent in an attempt to avoid the harsh metal of the heavily levered bit. His ears are reversed towards the rider in a gesture of resistance and discomfort. The near foreleg is extended flat-hooved in utter defiance, anchored to the spot, with the offside foreleg raised, ready to stamp with impatience. The great bronze balls of the stallion hang heavy, redolent, on the underside. This is a frozen moment steeped in will, testosterone and dangerous equine energy. And the king? The king is unconcerned, solid in his seat, sceptre in the right hand, double reins loose and looping to the bit in the left.

This is a portrait of control, of mastery over beast and dominion.

As a statement of equine nature it is just a little overstated. The truth, after 6000 years of selective breeding and a dozen conflicting sciences of submission and duty, is little more prosaic, almost ovine.

The horses you see grazing sleepily in the typical agistment paddock are more long-term detainees than free spirits of the plains. The males will be castrated and consequently dull. The whole herd, captives from birth, will show behaviour conditioned almost utterly by their interactions with humans and the degree of distress, trauma or well-fed content that they have brought.

And yet, at a whisper from the grass, at a secret sign from the sky, their minds will shrug off the burden of man and all the ages, and they will run like the wind. Lost in the moment. Almost free.

Island Bream

John Harms

I think of Fraser Island every day.

True.

I am reminded of it each morning by a simple oil painting that hangs on our bathroom wall. Sometimes, when I am riding the kids to get them ready for the day ('Get your shoes on, have you done your teeth, I'll get a new toilet roll'), I catch a glimpse of the painting and think of Fraser's tranquillity, her forget-the-worries-of-the-world isolation, and her beauty.

And I think about *Acanthopagrus australis*. The bream. A sleek silver fish, oval-ish in shape, a little longer than a school ruler, which zips around, here and there, in the gutters along the beaches of most of Australia.

The painting is of Indian Head, the rocky outcrop up the northern end of the island, on the eastern side, the first real interruption to a wide Pacific beach that stretches for almost 100 kilometres. It was painted, in his naive style, by a mate of mine, PJ, for many years a Mooloolaba dentist, and still going, whose family have enjoyed Fraser for half a century—from the 1960s, when all you'd find was a handful of laconic fishermen trying to keep their favourite spots secret.

I first met PJ when I had just enrolled at uni in Brisbane. He didn't attend as such, I don't think, it was more that he hung around. He was from the Sunshine Coast, where he spent a happy boyhood surfing until his father, Paul, the dentist at Nambour, realised his third child could only be saved by the brothers at Nudgee College. Off he trudged. As a boarder, PJ learned rugby and indolence.

One of the blessings of varsity and college life is it gives the like-minded a chance to find each other. We were from all over Queensland but each had found our own path to indolence. PJ didn't live at Union College, with many of us, but he was always at the Rec Club, enjoying the delights of multi-ball pinball ('Destroy Centaur'), drinking rum and Coke—Bundy, of course—and singing Daddy Cool's 'Bom Bom' with the covers band.

He was a good conversationalist with a wealth of experience. He had many theories. He believed a bloke should only own one pair of shoes. He preferred the ripple-soled golf shoes, which he wore to uni balls at Cloudland, at court appearances, to nightclubs (always thongs to the pub), and on the West Course at Indooroopilly.

I don't think I knew PJ was studying dentistry until he offered to make Madge, the toothless barmaid at the Royal Exchange in Toowong, a set of dentures. ('That'd be bonzer, darl.') I reckon he was in fourth year. Madge, who'd been around, and who knew your school's order before you got to the bar, was pleased as punch.

I also didn't know of PJ's deep affection for Fraser Island. He was one of those students who'd duck off for a surf regularly, but his family often went to Fraser—the whole lot of them besotted by the place—whether the fish were biting or not. They had an old four-wheel drive and they stayed in some ancient shacks.

Regulars on a favourite stretch of beach near Yidney Rocks, they became friends with one of the old blokes who lived by himself at Poyungan Rocks, on the beach just to the south. There is very little freehold land on Fraser, but Reg Rabies, a retired cocky from out west, who could have been any age from fifty-six to seventy-eight in that weathered outback Queensland way, actually owned a block. He had no one to pass it on to when he went to God. He wanted the block to go to a family who genuinely loved Fraser, so he did a deal with PJ's dad: if they kept him in motor vehicles, they would eventually own the title of the land.

That was a tougher deal than it first seemed. Fraser is harsh on four-wheel drives. The salt corrodes the metal. But the more immediate danger is the tide. To get around on Fraser, you drive along the beach, which is like the Gold Coast Highway for much of the day, but shrinks to nothing in many places at high tide. You can get caught. Many a proud (but inexperienced) owner has watched as their Jeep or Toyota has been sucked into the ocean by the surf. It is embarrassing, and expensive. Rule one at Fraser: know the tide times.

Old mate was a little careless with cars, and after a number were caught in the waves and last seen heading for New Caledonia, PJ's dad suggested a different arrangement. Rather than keep him in cars, they kept him in beer and looked after his medical prescriptions. Eventually the poor old bugger died.

His block was right on the beach. PJ's family built a simple, functional two-level shack with a couple of bedrooms—one with a double bed and one with about ten bunk beds in it. The upper level has a balcony, which looks out across the magnificent Pacific Ocean.

I didn't know about Poyungan in those days. PJ went to London and played up like a second-hand Victa, but returned a very capable dentist. The transition amazed most of us. We were battling away ourselves but, by the mid 1990s, most of us had taken enough steps along life's path to be able to organise our own time (with a bit of warning). So, we would respond to PJ's annual call. He'd nominate the week, put together the touring party, and off we'd go.

A party of old uni mates is a good (and dangerous) thing. We'd come from all over and meet at PJ's in Maroochydore. A couple of four-wheel drives would be stacked with the essentials—fishing gear, and enough supplies to cater for our rehydration—and off we'd go.

It was all about the fishing. (Really?) Fraser is famous for tailor, a fish that arrives at the island en masse. When they're running—in late winter—people stand shoulder to shoulder on the beach, reeling them in.

We toured in quieter times, times of fewer fish, in search of bream. We've always had our spots. Like the wreck of the *Maheno*, a ship that ran aground on the east side not far from Poyungan in 1935. It has attracted bream and other species ever since.

After crossing the Noosa River, we'd head along the mainland beach, past Double Island Point and Rainbow Beach, and on to Inskip Point, where we'd catch the barge to make the short crossing across shallow water to Fraser Island.

Then we'd drive along the beach and around the infamous Hook Point, which has caught many an unsuspecting driver. I recall seeing the expansive beach for the first time—wide, on low tide, it went forever. The late-spring light. The heat in the midday sun. The rich blue of the ocean. The huge sky. The white water of the crashing surf. And its sound. The massive dunes of the island, some gouged by the previous high tide, some like waves of perfect sand, some dotted with pandanus and casuarina trees and other vegetation. The beach, so flat, better than any paved city freeway, except for the many little creeks that leave the dunes and drain into the ocean.

Fraser Island is a paradise. It is a sand island. The inland lakes—especially Lake McKenzie—have to be seen to be believed. The water is pure, so clean, it's hard to gauge how deep it is. The stands of giant satinay and scribbly bark, among many other species, make a canopy, and rainforest. Fraser is filled with animal life. It's nothing to spot a sandy coloured goanna the size of a small crocodile. The bird life is majestic. Sitting at PJ's, you can watch the brahminy kites arc high into the sky. There are dingoes, and for a long time, there were mobs of brumbies.

The tours are always brilliant, but I remember one absolute cracker in the late 1990s. I was struggling (generally) to find the motivation to keep going with postgraduate research. I was sitting in the Fryer Library at the University of Queensland, looking at microfilm of 1930s newspapers, when on the screen appeared a news item about the sinking of the *Maheno*. 'Ah, Fraser Island,' I lamented.

And then: 'What an idiot I am. What on earth am I doing sitting in a dark library when I could actually be on Fraser?'

The incident became the catalyst to thrust my name before the selector (PJ) for a new tour.

That tour proved popular. There was BSN (a sort of forty-something Ferris Bueller), Sheeds (the vet), Big Trev (another dentist), Aldo (the pilot) et al. A fine bunch. It was the tour we had beach sprints, and played some dune golf with royal and ancient sticks; the tour when Rogan Josh won the Melbourne Cup.

There was no debate about the day's schedule. A post-sunrise fish out the front or at the *Maheno*—for bream—followed by pan-fried bream for brekkie. Maybe an early ale. A rest. A swim, perhaps, to get the hair salty and the skin feeling like you're on holidays. A drive along the beach to find pipis (*Paphies australis*)—some for lunch and some for bait. Pipis surface after a wave; the slightly raised wet sand at water's edge is the indicator. 'Pipis!' someone yells, causing PJ to come to a screaming halt—then it's dig, dig, dig.

A heap of pipis in chilli, white wine and lime juice, cooked in the wok over the wood fire in the yard, washed down with a nice Riesling. A little more Riesling. A book and a rest. A game of 500. Dodgy phone coverage and no thought of the internet; a blessing. PJ and BSN sorting out the fishing tackle, and driving up and down the beach in search of the right gutters. Some yabby-pumping and some wriggling in the sand for worms to augment the supply of pipis. Who knows what a bream fancies in the late afternoon.

Then three hours of can-in-hand (XXXX, of course) fishing.

The bream is the Corolla Seca of fish. It may not be a big fish, and it may not be the most defiant or sporty fish, but it's playful enough, especially for the once-a-year angler whose eyesight makes baiting a hook a victory in itself. I don't have PJ's touch—he's been known to wade in and grab fish with his hand—or BSN's determination, but I know how to celebrate when a decent glistening bream is dangling from the line. And when PJ does the honours on the cleaning table at home and he's preparing the catch for dinner. What follows is always conversation with blokes thinking they're funnier than they are, the red having performed its duty, until a few Bundies and a game of Rickety Kate fill the room with more laughter.

I have many memories of glorious Fraser afternoons when I look to the south or the north and see half a dozen of us spread along a pristine beach, golden sun behind us, favourite old T-shirts hanging over even older shorts, trying to outsmart a bream. These are some of the characters with whom I have lived my life. I just don't see them often enough.

I thank Fraser Island for getting us together. And I thank the humble bream.

Rescue Dog

Malcolm Knox

We went to the animal shelter for a cat and came away with Bruce.

The cat was the sensible idea. Two young children whose commitment to caring for a pet was untested against their enthusiasm for the idea of one. Two parents who had enough going on. So, yes, a cat: low-maintenance relationship, starter pet, family on trial.

But at the shelter that bright Saturday morning, the cats seemed to sense our commitment phobia and gave as little as they got. They said *miaow*, we said *meh* and found ourselves in the dog section.

There is no sadness like dog-shelter sadness. Instead of lively, love-starved puppies we found a gallery of invalids and discards, weepy-eyed mongrels who had been around the block once too often yet not often enough. Our experience, browsing from cage to soul-destroying cage, was akin to potential foster parents visiting an orphanage to find their choices narrowed to mature-aged divorcees, incurable gambling addicts and generationally unemployed chain smokers. You want to be a good person, but can you be that good? You want to be able to start a life, not steward a comfortable decline. I wish we could have had large enough hearts to take home a PTSD, arthritic, reeking spaniel-terrier cross with, literally, a kicked-dog expression when it could bring itself to look dolefully out of its cage.

We kept moving, propelled by guilt and melancholy, until we arrived at an empty cage with a name taped above it: BRUCE.

'Who's Bruce?' we asked the volunteer worker.

Her face lit up. 'Ah, Bruce. He'd be outside.'

We found Bruce in the fresh air. He was pulling another volunteer on a lead down a slope towards the shelter, or, as we would have it, towards us. Bruce was a six-month-old bundle of charisma with a kelpie's bod and a blue heeler's winsome eye-patches. Liquid brown eyes and chick-magnet grin. He had us at hello.

'You're lucky,' the handler said. 'If nobody took him this weekend, I was going to take him myself.'

I was back at the shelter on the Monday, the completed paperwork and a cheque for $280 in my pocket. Driving along Pittwater Road, I tempered my excitement to slow down through several speed-camera zones. Then it was up Mona Vale Road into semi-rural Ingleside, a hinterland off Sydney's northern beaches that houses nearly every animal shelter north of the city, like a specialised shopping district.

Riding shotgun was Greg Greene. We had moved into our house as a family of four. Six months on, we had acquired Greeny, and today we were adding Bruce.

Greeny was excited too. It was good to see him looking revived. Greeny is ten years older than me, and I have known him since

I was at school. The first house I moved into as a renter, for a six-month period back in the 1980s, was under Greeny's lead tenancy. A worldly law and maths graduate, he had been a kind of life mentor to my friends and me; we had remained friends as he broke the ground for us, into the thirties, forties and fifties, ten years ahead, like an advance party.

In the early autumn of 2009, soon after we moved into our house, I had made a routine phone call.

'Hey, Greeny, how's it going?' Rhetorical question, phatic communication, no reply necessary.

'Not so good, actually.'

Greeny, now fifty-three, was living with his 80-year-old mother in her retirement village unit. He had split with his long-term partner, who owned the house they had shared for a decade, and been kicked out. Amid his crisis he had lost, or walked out on, his job, and had no idea what he was going to do next. He had also lost his driver's licence for DUI. And he needed a shoulder reconstruction. Actually, not so good.

'Well,' I said, 'if you need anywhere to get some respite, you know we have a granny flat, and you're welcome to use it ...'

'That's all right,' Greeny said. 'Thanks for the offer, I appreciate it, but I'm fine with the old lady.'

'... for a weekend,' I finished my sentence, as Greeny spoke over the top of me.

The offer, and the decline, were almost Japanese: ritual forms of polite conversation, small talk between old friends, not statements with genuine will or content.

Or so I thought, until a week later, when Greeny called.

'You know what you said about your granny flat?'

Five months on, Greeny had put down deep roots in the flat. Still without job or licence, he had installed a fridge and a microwave and turned our outbuildings into a Kaczynski-ish hermitage. Sometimes he failed to emerge for days. He couldn't have been more ensconced in that flat if he'd been on witness protection. Occasionally he tiptoed past the house to slip out the side entrance, as if he could make himself invisible to us, but the more quietly he slinked, the more he was noticed.

On the upside, his shoulder had been successfully reconstructed.

We who lived in the main house had discussed the possible impact of the Bruce situation on Greeny, and couldn't see anything but positives. Although he was fundamentally a cat guy—when I lived with him, he had two beloved Burmese, Leon and Pris, as in *Blade Runner*—Greeny had expressed enthusiasm about our getting a dog. Taking Bruce for a walk, we reasoned, might get Greeny out of the granny flat for an hour a day and give him a much-needed (so we thought) sense of contributing to family life. Or, if he couldn't tolerate Bruce, it might well prompt him to get a job and move out. In other words, win-win.

So: Monday, midwinter 2009, Greeny and I rolled up to the animal shelter at Ingleside. I had bought a dog harness so that Bruce could sit on the comfortable imitation-leather back seat, rather than in the skanky back hatch area, for the ride to his new home.

'*Bruce*,' Greeny said as we parked. 'Is he a Bruce kind of dog?'

He was now. Bruce hadn't necessarily been my wife's name of choice for a family dog, but we had spent the weekend spooling through alternatives and nothing had suited that kelpie–cattle dog blokey bloke's dog quite so well. A Bruce by any other name ...

The animal welfare people shed tears while saying goodbye to Bruce. He panted and grinned and wagged his tail as we took him to the car and clipped him into his harness (at which, on my harness debut, I went through various permutations of legs and holes until I got Bruce right, reminding myself of a university lecturer I once had who had managed to convert a bench-pressing apparatus on a Nautilus machine into something on which she lay on her front while flexing her quadriceps; everyone else in the gym was too nonplussed, and amused, to set her straight).

God knows what Bruce thought of this display, and God knows what Bruce has thought of us ever since. What do dogs think? Although I grew up with dogs, I have always been very sceptical about anthropomorphising their thoughts and emotions. Does a wagging tail really mean a dog is happy? Do dogs really smile, or are their faces a funhouse mirror, a pathetic fallacy of resemblance as we smile back at them? Dogs bark when they are hungry, of course, or want to come inside on a winter night, and they do the pathetic flattened-eared mope when they are ill or seeking forgiveness. But other than that, I read dogs as I read wines: the extremes are obvious but the massive middle is a mystery. And I defy others to say they understand a dog's mind or moods. I don't even know if we have the right to call them 'he' or 'she', as if they have gender as well as sex. My brother, a veterinarian, thinks much the same, in a more rough and clinical way. They only have signs, he says, not symptoms. Not only can you not know a dog's thoughts, you cannot even know its capacity to think. You don't know its ability to remember. Ninety-nine point nine per cent of the emotional connection between dog and man comes from man. Which is why they're our best friend. They're the one relationship that forces us to give more than we receive, the one friendship where we must do all the emotional heavy lifting and supply all the affect. Whether we give a lot or a little, with dogs we are always giving the most. They are good for us in the way charities are good for the giver: a monstrously selfish altruism.

That said, Greeny and I didn't have to be dog whisperers to realise that Bruce was not having a happy car ride. We were not even out of Ingleside and onto Mona Vale Road before Greeny was raising his nose, sniffing the breeze and swivelling from the passenger seat.

'Bruce, no!' Greeny turned to me. 'He's puking.'

Smelling it before seeing it, I lowered the windows, but for every litre of fresh air blowing into the car, a cupful of spew was jetting out of Bruce, standing on the back seat with his back arched as he convulsed, the harness now acting as a choker.

'Should we stop?' Greeny said.

'It's only twenty minutes home,' I said, thinking I didn't have any towels or paper to mop up, and to stop and buy some would only prolong the agony. 'He can't have much more in him, I've got to make a run for it.'

I was wrong. By the intersection of Mona Vale and Pittwater roads, Bruce had emptied his stomach four or five more times. Somehow each vomit brought forward new reserves, as if he were the commander of an inexhaustible Red Army. Greeny was holding tight in the passenger seat, his gills trout-skin green, looking no better than the broken man who five months earlier had moved his refugee roll-on into the granny flat.

'Jeez, Bruce!'

I didn't need to turn around to know what Greeny was seeing now. By Warriewood, Bruce was going from both ends. The lagoon of vomit on the floor was being fed by a creek of diarrhoea dripping off the edge of his seat. I used to do this, when I was a kid; it was due to the new-car smell. This car wasn't new. Maybe for Bruce it was a new-family smell.

Safe to say, Bruce wasn't very happy on that drive. But what was the species of his unhappiness? Memory? Pavlovian reaction to being in a closed space, some recollection of abuse? In times to come, Bruce would freak out, barking and yelping inconsolably, if ever we went into an echoing concrete space such as an underground car park or the entrance to our local supermarket. What buried trauma was triggered by those cold vaults, by that back seat? Was Bruce remembering something in our car, or was it purely the moment, the panic and revulsion at strange motion and unaccountable smells?

We project much of our notion of 'intelligence' onto animals, but we cannot know where their senses and minds operate in relation to ours. Not only might they be unhappy when we think they are happy, and vice versa, but their happiness and unhappiness might run on different coordinates, in a different dimension. Their minds may be more rudimentary than ours by any degree; they may also have a completely extra-human perception—for all we know, they might be able to intuit the future. If we think they are less intelligent but more happy than us, they might be the converse: more knowing and filled with dread.

What if Bruce was seeing into the future? He might have seen the day, a few weeks hence, when I would take him for a run while riding my bike, and he ducked in front of my wheel so that I ran him over, gashing his hind leg and necessitating a trip to the vet for stitches that cost us $350, which made him, in automotive economic terms, a write-off.

Or was he seeing a future where he would be loved and neglected by our children in equal measure, hugged and adored and patted and all too frequently forgotten-to-be-fed and unwalked? Was he seeing the inevitable hours of loneliness, when nobody would be at home to give him his kitchen-sink drama to watch through the back door? Could he see the six-month period when we would, finally, own a cat (Bobby McGee, a hand-me-down from a hand-me-down from a hand-me-down, eventually lobbing with us via my wife's mother)? Could Bruce, while shitting and puking in the car, somehow sense the violent hatred with which Bobby would respond to his attempts at play? Was the presentiment of rejection making Bruce sick? Or the presentiment of Bobby's death, under the wheels of a passing car, and his subsequent karmic burial in the backyard that Bruce would restlessly patrol like a cemetery guard?

I can't say what Bruce saw while he was projectile-vomiting and shitting on the back seat. I can't say he didn't already see right through me to the type of dog owner I was, and knew that I would get so exasperated with his habit of chewing up tennis balls or losing them in the local lagoon that I would unleash the most vitriolic personal abuse upon him and call him names that no dog deserves to be called. Perhaps he was seeing the kind of master I would be towards him, feeding him and walking him and letting him inside, sometimes happily, sometimes grudgingly; but he was also caught in the grip of the genetically programmed loyalty he would show me, having designated me as pack leader, a baton I never asked for and didn't merit. The tragedy of fealty sworn to the undeserving: Bruce's future would make you want to puke.

Or perhaps he was seeing the holidays he would spend at my parents' house, three squares a day, a toastie or morning tea, and a warm berth in front of a heater every afternoon and evening. Perhaps he saw all the things we would believe made him happy: runs in the park, meetings with other dogs, more runs, more dogs, more arses to sniff, more balls to chase, more filthy ponds to swim in and puddles to lie in, more home-cooked meals, more raw meals, more family holidays, more belonging, more treats, more pats—and maybe foreseeing all this love was what was making him sick. Maybe a dog is a Sartrean existentialist. *La Nausee*: hell is other people.

Greeny and I were other people, in the front seat, given our own twenty minutes of hell in the miasma of Bruce's secretions. Greeny would hold out in the granny flat for another five months, long after he got a job and regained his driver's licence. Bruce would go absolutely nuts whenever Greeny came home, hurling himself at him and scraping his dirty paws down Greeny's front. Greeny would shout 'Bruce! Bruce, down! *No!*' while vigorously flapping his hands at chest level, as if working a pump. I think I could read Bruce's mind. He was hearing Greeny saying, 'Bruce! Bruce! Jump up at my hands! Great to see you! *Yes!*'

Or maybe Bruce just wanted Greeny to move out, so he could have his space to himself. Greeny's weekend respite turned into nine months by the end, and his intentions were often as opaque as those of Bruce, who now sleeps in what was Greeny's kitchenette and study.

And Greeny never took him for one walk.

A week after driving Bruce home, I went to the letterbox and found that on that trip from Ingleside I had broken the speed limit in a school zone by more than 15 kilometres per hour and was now several hundred dollars and three demerit points poorer.

That was seven years ago. Today he is curled by my feet. His ears are pricked: he sleeps like a dog. To humans, he is a devilishly handsome beast, and all who know him comment on what a lovely, loving, sweet-natured dog he is. When I walk him, I have a halter on his snout, because even though he is a seven year old, a senior dog, he is still a puppy at heart and would pull my arm out of its socket if he saw a cat or a rabbit. Sometimes on walks a parent will wrench their child away from Bruce, sheep in wolf's clothing, and warn, 'Don't go near that dog, it has a muzzle.' I leap indignantly to Bruce's defence, explaining that a halter is not a muzzle and he is not a biter, the halter is only to make up for my own inadequacies. If they remain frightened, I am quick to anger on Bruce's behalf. Humans are the strangest beings, but I guess we all see what we want to see.

I dearly hope Bruce's is a happy life, if happiness is a thing for dogs. Whenever he gives us what we think is a smile, we joke that he is thanking us for getting him out of that animal shelter. But we can't know. Getting into that car was his moment of destiny, when his roulette wheel slowed and his ball fell into chance's slot. He found himself with me and Greeny. At such a vertex, who would not feel sick?

Stud

Garry Linnell

The Irish boys are putting on helmets and tightening leather straps. The boss is squeezing his scrubbed hands into a pair of germ-free latex gloves. The room is heavy with the odour of antiseptic lotion. It can only mean one thing: love is in the air.

And so it is time for Stick Man to go to work. Adrian O'Brien, Stick Man's boss, enters his stall. 'C'mon, lad, time to go,' he says, patting his charge on the rump. The Stick knows this routine off by heart. If a horse could shrug, he'd be doing it now.

It's late on a warm spring afternoon at the elite Coolmore Stud, deep in the Hunter Valley. In the next few minutes the brutal efficiency that lies at the heart of the global, multibillion-dollar thoroughbred industry will be on display. But first, Stick Man, a 9-year-old white pony with the tousled mane of an 1980s rock star, must do what he does best—start a job he always leaves half-done.

O'Brien, tall, freckled and with the clinical demeanour of a surgeon, leads Stick Man out of his stall and into the vast breeding barn. Waiting there, shifting nervously, is Tempest Morn, a plain brown mare.

Trained by Gai Waterhouse, owned by the Filipino brewing billionaire Eduardo Cojuangco, and with a reputation for courage on the track, Tempest Morn won two Group One races. Now she's a sex object. She arrived only a few minutes ago, trucked in from Mudgee. She was taken straight into a padded stall, where O'Brien bandaged her tail before wiping down her rear with a sterilising solution. The indignities only grew worse. Led into the cavernous mating arena, with its soft light, peaked ceiling, padded walls and freshly laid woodchip floor, she had thick felt boots strapped to her rear feet by two of O'Brien's assistants. She hated that, kicking out in a hopeless attempt to remove them.

Now one of her amber eyes is widening as Stick Man approaches. A groom tightens the twitch—a stick with a loop of rope at the end that is twirled around her upper lip. The twitch is supposed to be a distraction, as well as a trigger to release a rush of pain-dulling endorphins. She shivers and whinnies.

In the horse-breeding industry, Stick Man is a teaser stallion, the warm-up man for the main act. But he's also the equine version of the royal food-taster. He gets to sample this and that, but a seat at the banquet will forever be denied him.

If Tempest Morn, about to experience her first mating, kicks out with those booted feet, it will be the Stick who takes the punishment, not the hundred-million-dollar thoroughbred being prepared a few hundred metres away in a separate barn.

Stick Man nuzzles her flanks and she calms a little. But when he rears, clearly aroused by her scent, she scurries sideways, avoiding him. The Stick flashes his teeth and moves forward again.

This time Tempest Morn allows him to land his forelegs on her back. He humps into fresh air.

O'Brien decides the mare is ready for the real stuff. He yanks on Stick Man's lead, and the pony dismounts. His erection disappears by the time he placidly leaves the arena. He might do this thirty times a day, maybe more. O'Brien is smiling. 'Good lad, good lad,' he says.

Now, Giant's Causeway is being led from his stall to the breeding barn. You can hear him long before you see him. Even from a distance, his primal roaring and bellowing is enough to make you swallow hard and take a step back. He's a liver chestnut with a white blaze on his forehead rising like a curl of smoke from just above his left nostril.

As he approaches the barn, his surging testosterone levels physically lift him. He rears like a motorcyclist on one wheel, forelegs flailing, punching the air. You can see why they nicknamed him 'The Iron Horse'.

This stallion won five Group One races as a three year old in Europe, but it was the manner of his victories that stunned everyone. Headed a few times in the straight and looking as if his fuel tank was empty, Giant's Causeway kept coming back, surging again. He has heart, just like the virgin waiting nervously for him in the barn.

Fear ripples through Tempest Morn's velvet coat. She doesn't know what is going on, but every instinct tells her she's about to find out. The choir of Irish voices in the room—Coolmore's world empire is based in Tipperary—returns to its favourite chorus: 'Good girl ... good girl ... be still now. Attagirl ... Attagirl ...'

Giant's Causeway's handler leads him towards the mare. The stallion's nose twitches. The barn falls silent.

O'Brien leans forward and pulls Tempest Morn's bandaged tail to one side. More silence.

And then it starts. The stallion, fully aroused, roars and rears high as his handler rushes to one side, pulling at the rein.

Then 500 kilograms of muscled horseflesh crashes onto Tempest Morn's back. Someone is yelling, 'Giddup, giddup, giddup.' Giant's Causeway's forelegs are splayed across the back of his mount. His head is shaking and tiny bits of froth are being flung from the corners of his mouth.

The four men below are moving quickly, like tiny stagehands. O'Brien, the mare's tail in one hand, is reaching under the stallion, grabbing the animal's penis and guiding it to the right spot. One of the helmeted assistants is straining against Tempest Morn's chest and shoulder to stop her from moving forward.

The groom with the twitch is out to one side, tightening its hold.

Giddup, giddup, giddup.

For twenty-five frantic seconds, the barn is filled with whinnying and human shouting and raucous horse farting as muscles spasm and spinal cords grind.

Giddup, giddup, giddup. Attagirl. Attagirl. Comeongirl, that's it. With one last thrust, Giant's Causeway, his feet still splayed awkwardly, falls silent. A bloodline stretching back more than three centuries has just been passed on at the cost of $137500. The stallion leans forward and nibbles gently at Tempest Morn's mane, caressing it almost affectionately with his teeth.

Then, with a final, tired heave, he dismounts. Moments later he is heading back down the lane for a feed and a roll in fresh straw. He doesn't look back.

Tempest Morn, still stunned, still with her tail in the air, is led out the rear door. She passes by Stick Man's stall on her way to an old blue truck outside. The Stick's left eye peers out through a tumbled mass of white hair and he watches her pass. For a brief moment, you imagine a flash of envy. But he quickly looks away when he spies you staring at him.

He doesn't want your pity. Stick Man just wants a little action.

....

Racing people often talk about the romance of the turf, but there's nothing romantic about the act that underpins it all. The ritual has all the intimacy and warmth of a visit to a dental surgery. It's brutal and swift, the closest the animal kingdom has come to simulating a date between Mike Tyson and a beauty pageant contestant.

'There's no foreplay and no afterplay,' says Brett Howard, Coolmore's sales manager.

'For most of them it's wham, bam, thank you, ma'am. As far as we're concerned, that suits us. If we have thirteen stallions operating, we like to keep them moving … like a production line.'

But there's another reason for the carefully choreographed routines and sterile surrounds. With hundreds of millions of dollars riding on such encounters—Kevin Conley, the author of *Stud: Adventures in Breeding*, declares the mating act the most expensive thirty seconds in sport—thoroughbred reproduction is an incredibly risky business. One stray wiry hair from Tempest Morn's tail could have cut Giant's Causeway's penis, potentially putting him out of action for weeks. With stallions mating up to three times a day throughout an Australian breeding season that lasts from 1 September until Christmas, losses can soon reach huge proportions.

These are not just reproductive machines but highly prized corporate assets worth tens of millions of dollars. You might wonder why, in an age of fabulous technological advances, when scientists claim to be on the cusp of bringing extinct species back to life, racing even bothers allowing its horses to procreate in the old-fashioned way.

Horse mating appears to be a clumsy, hit-and-miss affair that, without the guiding hand of a stallion manager, leaves you wondering how the species has managed to survive the past 55 million years since *Eohippus* first appeared in the Eocene epoch. Other sports that use animals long ago jumped on the safety-first artificial insemination bandwagon. Some of the world's greatest trotting sires are technically still virgins, mounting wooden pommel horses and ejaculating into sterile containers in order for their genes to be flown to all corners of the globe. And it's not as if the sport is run by Luddites—horses are DNA tested to certify their breeding credentials, and thoroughbreds at the track are regularly scrutinised for the tiniest quantities of performance-enhancing drugs.

But the industry remains defiant—and not just because the stud ritual is somehow romantic. Here's the rub: artificial insemination would topple the breeding market and financial empires created by the multinational entities that dominate the sport. The world's top sires work in both hemispheres and command stud fees approaching $US500 000. Imagine how those fees might tumble if just a little bit of that sperm went a much longer way. 'The market would be ruined,' says one breeder. 'You would be flooded with the foals of the world's best sires and the industry would collapse.'

And Stick Man would find himself out of a job, no longer in charge of unfinished business at Coolmore.

Shepherds

William McInnes

Peewee was a bit crook. That's what the old bloke with the thick-bottle-lens glasses said to the young woman behind the counter at the vet clinic. Said it very slowly in an old man's voice, deep and furry. 'Yes, poor old Peewee's seen better days.'

'So he's a bit unwell,' said the young woman.

'That'd be why he's here, I'm afraid. He makes me look like Johnny Weissmuller and I've got more rot in me than a house full of borer.'

The young woman smiled a little and asked who Johnny Weissmuller was.

The old man tilted his head back. 'That shows me age, doesn't it? Tarzan. He makes me look like Tarzan.'

And he pulled gently at the ears of his old dog, Peewee. I think he was a fox terrier and he looked as old as Moses.

I don't know what it is about old men and old dogs, but looking at them across the waiting room it was almost as if I couldn't imagine them ever being any other age.

But they must have been. The old bloke must once have been a little boy watching a Tarzan movie starring Johnny Weissmuller as the king of the jungle.

Now he gently pulled at his old dog's ears as he waited for Paddy the vet to call him in. He was next in line and my daughter and our two little puppies were after him.

I held Ray and my daughter held Delilah. I'm not sure how they got their names but they sort of suit them.

Ray Delilah. If you run the names together it sounds like a winger from the Valley Diehards in the BRL in the 1970s.

We weren't really holding the pups; it was a case of juggling the little kelpies, as all they wanted to do was tear around the crammed waiting room.

People and their pets.

Apart from Peewee and the old bloke, there was a man with Nina, the fuzz-ball German shepherd puppy. She was cute, as most puppies are, but I had a history with German shepherds.

When I was a kid, we would indulge in a little thrillseeking on a lazy Saturday morning by engaging in a little Karl racing.

We lived next door to a fire station, and through its grounds was the short cut to the BP servo on the corner, which had a small stand, filled with treasure—jelly snakes, fruit gums and chewing gum. The chewy was the most sought-after pleasure because, for some reason, the selection was huge. Besides the Wrigley's PK, Juicy Fruit and Spearmint, there was a collection of gum called Beachies, which came in musk, grape and peppermint. Along with that lot was a lower shelf that was like a chewy bazaar, where you could find Big Charlie gum sticks, Black Cat blocks and Bazooka Joes.

All this lolly currency was wagered and traded between us kids. And Karl was the opponent. Karl was a psychotic German shepherd that would occasionally prowl the fire station grounds.

Karl belonged to one of the officer's sons, a young man with cerebral palsy and quite a few pets. He kept pigeons in a coop by the incinerator in the fire station and would occasionally bring along the family cat, a great ginger tom with a happy, lazy face. And, of course, there was always Karl.

'They make him feel happy,' said my mother, 'and that is a gift.'

Even Karl. It never once occurred to me that Karl could be an affectionate companion, for to all of us kids he was the instrument of chance and fate, a four-legged furry roulette wheel, with teeth.

'Going out to race Karl,' one of us would say, for no particular reason; then it was on.

'Betcha you don't make it past the bomb shelter.'

'Betcha I can.'

'Betcha you can't.'

'Betcha a packet of Beachies Musk I can.'

I was the youngest by six years and easy prey for Karl but had enough Irish in me to love to bet up big.

I seldom made it past the bomb shelter, a strange round brick building that had been built in the 1950s as a training facility for the firemen, but was given its nickname by my mother.

So, I would lose lots of Beachies.

One morning, though, I didn't even make it to the bomb shelter. I was, it must be admitted, carrying a lot of weight—a Big Charlie stick, a packet of Black Cats and a Beachies Musk all crammed in my Stubbies shorts' odd little front pocket—as I ran through the grounds.

Karl came from nowhere and I had no choice but to leap up on the sharp wire netting of the tennis courts in the fire station grounds. The metal dug into my fingers and toes, while, below me, Karl leaped and snarled.

These courts were open to public hire and a game of doubles was in full swing. A big woman in a small hat with a visor, and a ballooning pleated tennis skirt that swirled like some sea anemone, was stalking the baseline in between serves.

'I could never, ever vote for the Whitlam fellow.' She paused, inspecting the balls, as I clung to the wire. 'He may not be a communist but I'm sure he's a socialist.'

She stopped and turned to look at me. She had green–black clip-on shades attached to her glasses, and I could see the whole scene reflected in her specs—me, Karl, and, staggering along, the officer's son, Karl's owner. He had a hold of his collar and was trying to quieten him but the big dog was shaking him like he was a toy.

I hung in her sunglasses for what seemed like ages, until I heard the boy say in his awkward way that it was all right to go, as Karl had calmed down. I jumped down, saw the boy was scratching the ears of the big dog, and walked, then ran, to the safety of our fence.

I heard the woman in the anemone skirt. 'A socialist!' she snapped as she hit the ball …

Back in the vet's waiting room, Nina the German shepherd puppy looked cute all right, but when I saw her I still felt the wire netting of the court on my fingers and toes.

I looked around the surgery.

A big grey cat called Biscuits was asleep in the arms of a young woman who was a walking monument to the age of punk. She had a safety pin through her eyebrow, dyed, spiky hair and the loveliest smile. There was a Vietnamese family with a budgie called Kevin, and a younger couple with another budgie, named Thor.

Paddy wandered from the consulting room and called out, 'Eric, you want to bring Peewee through?'

Eric got up slowly. The punk, still cuddling Biscuits, stood and offered a hand.

'Cheers, love,' said Eric and rolled into the consulting room.

He was very old.

I suppose a lot of people don't see the point of pets. It doesn't make them bad people. Likewise, the fact some people make money from pets does not make the pets bad. They're still pets, even if they are mass-produced 'designer pets', which some might see as making them just another decoration or accessory. It says a lot more about the shallowness of the owner than about any shortcomings of the pet. Once, probably when a young Eric watched Johnny Weissmuller play Tarzan, pets ate the scraps from their owners' tables; now the pet food industry is worth tens of millions of dollars.

But sitting in a room with a bunch of people and their pets makes me feel okay. I remember that crazy German shepherd and his owner. Karl wasn't mad all the time. Not long after I was hanging suspended, reflected in the glasses of the woman with the anemone skirt, I heard the boy laughing. I was lounging in the hammock on our side veranda, and looked out and saw him playing with Karl. The big dog was shoving his head against his owner's and nuzzling for a cuddle.

'They make him feel happy,' my mother had said about the boy's pets, 'and that is a gift.'

The tenderness that people show their pets makes us all a little better.

But, all in all, I'm still not sure about German shepherds.

A Boy and His Dog

Shaun Micallef

When I was very young—I must have been about eight or nine—I had an imaginary dog. At least, I'm told it was imaginary. My mother assures me I did not have a real dog until I was fourteen: a black-and-white sort-of-kelpie called Jerry that I didn't like very much because he was crazy.

I remember Jerry well because he'd bark a lot and chase the spores that rays of sunlight lit up as they streamed through my bedroom window while I was trying to study in the afternoons. He'd yap at them and jump on my bed and I'd have to take him outside and throw a tennis ball at him until he'd settle. Yeah, I remember him—but this other dog I remember just as well was a different one. A light brown, almost yellow, labrador that was very calm and used to lay his head in my lap while I was reading and smile when I stroked his head. The memory is vivid—but, as I say, my mother assures me we never had a dog apart from Jerry.

Now, I know memories are notoriously unreliable but, for a while, I simply couldn't believe that Tim (that was the dog's name) had never existed. My mother is quite elderly and I wondered at first whether it was *her* memory that couldn't be trusted. But she told me I certainly used to talk to her about Tim when I was young: she thought at the time it must have been a dog I played with on the way home from school; that is, until she found me 'playing' with him in the backyard.

Apparently I was running about and laughing and hugging the air and throwing sticks and worrying everybody unnecessarily. I'm not sure who the 'everybody' was but the lady from the NHSA didn't seem too bothered by it when my mother took me in and made me tell her about our adventures. I was quite happy to relay one or two of our more dangerous escapades and, at her request, even draw a picture of the most hair-raising one with the special soft crayons she had called Cray-Pas (a small packet of which I was allowed to keep).

It was the time Tim and I crossed that river. Of course, there was no river at all near my suburban Adelaide home; there was a storm drain and there was a creek up at Brown Hill but nothing that resembled the raging torrent that almost swept Tim and me away.

A few years ago, though, when I was cleaning out my parents' shed (preparatory to putting them in a home or maybe an asylum), I came across a box of mouldy old comics. These were the *Phantom* ones I didn't really like much but were quite cheap and so were what I bought with my six-cents-a-week pocket money. I was disappointed my father hadn't looked after these more carefully because this collection, if pristine and not a damp mass of papier-mâché, would have fetched plenty on eBay. But that was my father: he'd already burned my first-edition *Rupert the Bear* albums because 'they were old'.

Inside the rotting comic book box, though, was a little red dog collar I distinctly remembered Tim wearing when we went looking for that prison escapee that time and that I had to cut off with my Barlow pocket knife when he got tangled in an elderberry bush. It was getting dark and we'd heard a noise we were convinced was the convict lurking in the shadows. Tim barked at me to run home and save myself but I certainly wasn't going to leave him behind to God knows what fate at the escapee's murderous hands. I whipped out my knife and hacked through Tim's collar, heart pounding so hard I could barely hear the thunder that cracked over us. Then the heavens opened up with a mighty *boom*! Whether it was the killer's bony hands on my shoulder—or perhaps just a stray branch—as soon as Tim was freed we bolted through the driving rain to safety.

Scrambling up the embankment, though, I tripped and struck my head on a rock and blacked out. Tim, way ahead and already trying to get under the barrier, came back to me, licking my face between flashes of lightning until I regained consciousness, then dragged me back to the road by the hood of my jacket and stood guard and barked at passing traffic until a kindly policeman stopped and took us home. My parents were sick with worry and my grandmother, whom I rarely saw because she was rich and lived on the other side of town in a big house that smelled of pine needles and Fabulon, was there too, with a block of peppermint chocolate for me to have when I felt better. But my mother said I wasn't allowed to eat it because I had scared her and my father half to death. So she ate it instead.

Tim had saved my life. He was a hero. In the real world he would have been awarded that medal for animal bravery they gave those dolphins in World War II.

The adult me showed the severed collar to my aged father, hoping he would be inundated with the same Proustian flood as I had. But no, he couldn't recall the incident and chuckled softly at the mention of my imaginary dog. He said the collar had belonged to Jerry and that it had been cut up when he ran over it with the lawnmower.

'But don't you remember we both went fishing with him that time?' I asked. I was sure we had. He thought a moment as he continued peeling an apple with a small knife (using only one hand; a skill I always admired but, sadly, never acquired).

When the peel was off he shook his head. 'No, no—that was Wolfie Leigh. And I couldn't come that day because I was working ...'

Wolfie Leigh. I hadn't thought about him in years. Wolfie's real name was not Wolfie, but Tony. We called him Wolfie because he had a single eyebrow and incisors that looked like fangs. He lived two houses down from us. His father had been a Spitfire pilot in World War II and during a mission his windscreen had been shot out by a Messerschmitt. His face was horribly disfigured. Wolfie's mother was much younger and quite beautiful, much more so than the other neighbourhood mothers and so, of course, none of the mothers liked her. Wolfie had a sister, too, and she had encephalitis. It was a strange family but Wolfie had a television set and we didn't so I spent a lot of time over there and we became pals, much to the consternation of my mother, who thought the Leighs were 'like something out of *Tales from the Crypt*'.

Wolfie and I had gone fishing at Brown Hill Creek without telling anyone. We'd just seen *The Adventures of Huckleberry Finn* at the pictures; we had been rather taken with it. Back at Wolfie's place, we made fishin' poles out of a broomstick and an old curtain rail and, barefoot despite the fact it was winter, with Wolfie in his mother's sun hat and me chewin' on what I thought was a piece of straw but was probably one of the long matches Captain Leigh used to light his pipe, we set out on our adventure. I guess I was Tom Sawyer because Wolfie had the freckles. With no bait or line or hook we caught very few fish but we did manage to get some tadpoles in a jar we found. And we got very muddy. We lost track of time and when it started to rain we took shelter under a bridge.

Meanwhile, our parents were frantic and had called the police. Captain Leigh had led a search party along the canal and into the big stormwater pipe, where no one was supposed to go. A little boy had been found in there once, we'd been told. There were never many details given but we assumed the poor boy had been found dead. True or not, it was *the* cautionary tale for children in our neighbourhood, solemnly recounted whenever a child was naughty.

The creek was swollen and the rain was beating down but Wolfie and I could still hear the voices of the adults as they crossed and re-crossed the stone bridge we were under. It was exciting. We wondered if we should stay where we were until they all went home, then reappear dramatically in the morning, perhaps even sneaking into our own funerals, like Tom in the movie. In the end, Captain Leigh shone a torch in our faces and Wolfie got a whipping.

I was spared anything like that. My mother and father sat with me in silence in the back of my grandfather's car as he drove us slowly home, my mother holding my hand, and my father's wet hat dripping on the picnic blanket they'd wrapped around me. My grandfather's fierce eyes looked at me now and then in the rear-view mirror but he said nothing. We weren't close. I saw him even less than I saw my grandmother. He was a policeman but, regrettably, he had brought his normal car ...

My father handed me a bit of apple and creaked back in his old chair, feet on the desk he used, his whole life, to sketch his designs (he was a commercial artist, responsible for the original drawing of the Coppertone girl in 1953).

'You used to like movies and comic books back then, didn't you?' he said. Sure, I did; they were my life. Adelaide in the 1960s was almost as dull as it is now. 'You remember what the Phantom called his dog?' Of course, I remembered. His name was Devil and he was a wolf.

My father fed himself another sliver of apple straight from the blade. 'And what was the other film on the bill that day you saw the one about Huck Finn?' I thought hard but couldn't remember. Dad went through the drawer in his desk and pulled from it a yellowing cut-out from the cinema section, an ad for *Old Yeller* starring Tommy Kirk. He was right. I'd cried when Old Yeller died but then, so did everyone—why had he kept it? Dad shrugged and smiled. 'I took you and Wolfie that day. We saw it together. It was your birthday, remember?' I hadn't. 'You had your heart set on a puppy and your mother and I gave you a copy of *To Kill a Mockingbird* instead. We went to the pictures to cheer you up.'

That's right, that's right. Of course, I read the book later and loved it—it was why I wanted to be a lawyer—but at the time I'd wanted a puppy just like the little one in my father's Coppertone ad.

'Remember what Old Yeller got bitten by?' my father asked, leaning back in the chair again. 'A wolf, wasn't it? It gave him rabies. That's why Tommy had to shoot him. And remember the name of the dog in *To Kill a Mockingbird* that Atticus shoots because he has rabies?'

Tim Johnson.

Dad nodded.

Tim.

Oh God. Old Yeller was a 'yellow' labrador that contracted rabies, just like Tim Johnson. I'd conflated my experience with Wolfie, and made Wolfie a dog through my association of him with the Phantom's wolf dog, *The Phantom* being written and drawn by Lee Falk—Lee as in Leigh, see? And I'd created a false memory of being rescued in the rain from the clutches of an evil stranger by a trusty and heroic, but completely imaginary, dog.

When in fact all I'd done was go to the pictures with my dad and my best friend and then get lost in a park. Even the trip home with the policeman was really just with my grandfather.

I've always been an impressionable lad. That night, I had dinner with my parents. My mother made flapjacks and hominy grits and Pop and me sat by the fire a'whittlin' and talkin' about that whole mess o' crawfish we was gonna catch the next day after church. Ma sang some old darkie work songs from the kitchen as she rustled up them vittles and just as the big ol' sun disappeared behind them big trees over yonder I looked down and there lyin' on the floor with his head in my lap was good ol' Tim, just as peaceful and a'smilin' as he were all them years ago.

I stroked his head and let him have a puff on my corn-cob pipe. 'This is the life, eh, Tommy,' he said.

'It's fine and all,' I replied, 'but I reckon I got to gits me out for a spell and head west, afore the Widow Douglas tries to adopt and sivilize me. I can't stand it, Tim. I been there before. I beeeeen there before.' And Tim laughed and shook his head.

At least, that's my memory of it.

Smiling in the Dark

Bruce Pascoe

An hour before dusk and the river vegetation is exhaling a dank brine. I breathe it in and watch; the correct way to approach a river in this country.

I flick a prawn into the deep shadow beneath the melaleuca. The line moves a fraction, just a tiny nudge. Stillness. The line moves again, slowly, heading for the bank. I strike and the rod curves with all the startled strength of a big bream. I tug the fish away from the submerged forest of snags and reel it in. I bring it up to the jetty and its eye is furious but soon dulls to confused acceptance of the drug it is breathing.

I slice the fillets off either side and turn to feed the frame to the pelican but he must have been off hunting with the family, so I snap the neck and toss the carcass into the river.

I watch it float and turn in the water. It's close to full tide, the flow is sluggish and the fish barely moves downstream. The stomach still has air in it and the frame drifts on the surface.

Fingerling mullet gather to fret and fray the skeleton. They are busy little fish and their communal effort makes the carcass jig and pitch: they are like tiny tugboats tending their big dead cousin.

Then the eel arrives. She covets any food in this part of the river. She has a small world of perhaps 70 metres at this time of her life but it is hers and she guards it with teeth like the needles of a nit comb.

She takes hold of the fish's tail and jostles it against the wattle trunk that fell into the river the flood before last. She nudges and pushes, trying to loosen flesh from the bones and then she wrenches and lashes her long body. The little mullet are not too alarmed. They work around the eel in relative safety: she scorns the amount such small fry consume.

The mullets' greater concern is the kingfisher, which has the habit of watching such river cameos then darting in to snip a slip of silver from the water and return to its perch, little fish flipping helplessly. The kingfisher's beauty belies its murders.

But the kingfisher has not long flown upstream and probably won't return before dark. Do the mullet know this? Have they seen the image of the disappearing bird blurred by the water and feel emboldened to feed on the bream carcass dandling so temptingly on the surface?

A stingray slides beneath the jetty and rises to inspect the activity on the surface. I expect the eel to turn on the stingray, gnashing its fearsome teeth, but the ray rises and glides past the dead fish and the eel writhes across its back but seems strangely deferential, perhaps nervous of the blade on the ray's tail.

The stingray repeats this manoeuvre and each time the eel slides, coiled, across its back while the fry remain unconcerned, continuing to tug at the edges of the bream.

Finally, the eel curves away to the murky light at the bottom of the river and disappears. The ray keeps making passes across the fish and I see no reason for it until I realise it's feeding on the mullet, positioning its mouth to scoop them up as they concentrate on their own meal.

The river is slow enough that I can still see the entire drama as if staged just for me. The eel, by bunting the bream carcass to the bank, has slowed the show down even more.

Still the ray makes its solemn passes and still the mullet scatter only to reform their frittering cloud like machinists in a sweatshop sewing factory.

The sky turns from lemon to rose then brick red with clumps of dark cloud looming.

I watch as the ray leaves and the eel sneaks back in sinuous and sullen curves to wrestle the dead fish, the river surface darkening to a gunmetal colour flecked with swatches of light like dirty silver spoons.

In this dim light I hear the first whooping and weirdly rollicking call of the nightjar. He must have roused himself from his hide among the carpet of round-leaf box leaves where he always sleeps, invisible among the tawny doubloons.

The bird glides by on flat wings as mysterious as the best of ghosts, dipping and curving and clipping evening insects from the air.

Soon it is too dark to see if the mullet are still feeding and the only indications that the eel is present are the sudden nudges and bunts of the fish's body, little surges of activity betraying the first flares of phosphorescence.

I can't leave the river when that ghost light is present so I tip over the *Whitehall Trader*, a rowboat as lean as a greyhound and as quiet as a fox. I call her Fluke, for the distinctive whale tail detail on her transom. I slip her onto water the colour of spilt ink. At the bow's entry a tube of hot green glass unspools like a ribbon on her flank. I find my seat, feeling buoyancy below me, and the thrill of entering another dimension.

My oars drip with phosphorescence, fish surge below me in a flare of light, and stars are fused to the water by their own brilliance. We are all blurred by this pale green blaze and the confusion of elements leaching into each other; a dream of water and midnight.

Mullet trail lime gauze as my oars spring spot fires and the boat leaves ribbons of green glass curving in its wake, a molten, ephemeral celebration of our passage.

The bow scrapes into the sand of the bank and I pretend to fish, knowing I don't need to drag another creature from its element. I watch as luminous fish creep to the bait then slink away into the deeper trenches of the river. I remove the prawn to avoid having to deal with a fish out of water. The water is so warm it's hard to know, when you slide your hand beside the boat, whether you are feeling water or glowing air.

A night heron lands beside the boat with a kwow of alarm, scandalised by my presence. He stalks away, indignation betrayed by pearls of light dripping from his skulking toes. This is *his* bank, his sanctuary; how dare I invade his murderous reverie.

The nightjar is still calling, as he has every night since the month warmed. That call mesmerised me as a young man. It took me years to see the maker of the whooping spook of sound. Eventually I saw him by moonlight and years later I disturbed his roost in a carpet of fallen leaves from the round-leaf box. The pattern of these layered circles of burnt red and jaded green is so reminiscent of my aunt's carpet that I always inspect it thereafter for the faint outline of a reclining bird and the half-opened defiance of its eye.

Every summer night I hear that call on the riverbank and spend hours waiting for the irregular return of its haunting as the stars wind down the sky, the Plough chasing Pleiades or, rather, the Seven Sisters fleeing across the sky from the spirit man who would treat them ill.

Cormorants have been flying into their roosts in the tree leaning above me. It's been dark for an hour but they know their way and now jostle and ruffle, settling for the night like a boarding house of boys braying like goats. I find myself smiling in the dark: a grown adult smiling at a riot of unruly friends.

I reverse from the bank, as Fluke is as easy to row backwards as forwards, and I slide across the deeper channel at the bend, 30 foot of black water in which skipjack streak like firework rockets, nervous of the depth and its denizens.

I wait.

At last I hear the grumble and bark of mulloway below me in the river's trench, too deep to allow phosphorescence to reveal the threat of their mass. The calls detonate on the hull like slow thunder. The river listens, the birds stilled by the lazy song of giants.

The journey home leaves an emerald boss of hot glass in our wake, a chevron uncoiling from the stern. The blades sweep and plunge, green fire skittering off each lifted blade. Coot and swamphen kek and cackle in the swamp, a pobblebonk frog gocks and clocks in its partly submerged cave, a marshy liquid tock.

The boobook's call is a slow and thoughtful repetition of its name as it blinks and stares, scaring the willies out of swamp rats and ring-tailed possums. The masked owl might not shriek tonight. She is sparing of her terror, and I have no grandfather to tell me if I should avoid her or luxuriate in her awful presence. But I need no grandfather to tell me that I am in love with the river of night and her dreadful conversations.

Cat Lovers

Liam Pieper

There's a story I tell when I want to look exotic and Antipodean, especially in front of strangers, and especially in front of Americans.

I struggle to feel truly Australian, or at least the kind of blue-eyed, blonde-haired, rugged-but-cheerful archetype marketed to the world in my youth. This was never on the cards for me; I'm slight, twitchy and genetically determined fittest to survive only if it depends on using gnarled little hands to dig potatoes out of a Celtic bog.

Cairns is the sort of town in which I feel my timidity keenly. The confluence of remoteness, hostile wildlife and climate (if someone has the temerity to build a house, it will quickly be claimed by a tornado) means the people who have settled there over the years tended to be first a blend of escaped colonial convicts and, later, escaped metropolitan convicts and, even later, hippies looking to live off the grid.

Their descendants are a unique hybrid of sunny New-Age optimism and seething murderous resentment.

'You look like a Capricorn,' a hulking, skinheaded goon in a sarong growled at me on the street on my first day in town. 'Don't fucking like Capricorns.'

I was in Cairns on holiday to visit my girlfriend Charlotte's family, because somewhere in my reptile brain I had realised that winning over the mother would help me hang onto the girl a little longer. Charlotte was very close with her mother. Her father was out of the picture—he lived in Canada, or Alaska, or Africa, maybe—someplace where men could hunt beasts of a weekend. Cairns had not been wild enough for him, perhaps.

Charlotte was beautiful, and, even worse, she was kind. Possessed of a slightly goofy small-town grace that not even years studying drama in New York, and then scraping by on bit parts in movies, could erode. Hollywood had somehow made her into a nicer person. She was kind to a fault and, back then, I responded to kindness exactly like a whipped dog does to treats. I would have followed her anywhere, even to Cairns, and I hoped that was enough.

I was, by any measure that mattered, not good enough for her. The disparity was most visible when we stood next to each other. She'd spent a childhood cavorting on beaches and eating mangos off the tree. I'd been a short, fat boy who lost weight by doing blow, so now I looked like a Shar-Pei pup. Sex was a logistical nightmare. Every time we made love I lost three Sherpas on the ascent.

Her family was similarly intimidating: huge, square-jawed, salt-of-the-earth types who drove giant utes with enclosed cages large enough for someone to stand up in. It was never explained to me exactly what they were used for.

Charlotte's people were rugged. They were handy. They were the sort of people who knew how to fix their cars, or gut a fish, or build an extension on their homes. They'd done the latter so often, adding an annex or an attic whenever the fancy took them, that Charlotte's mother's home had evolved into a sprawling red-brick mansion. A wooden porch overlooked a lap pool, beyond which lay a half-acre of tropical garden, which gave way to jungle beyond that. Somewhere in the distance the ocean rumbled—menacingly, I thought, but to be fair, I found nearly everything in the town menacing.

Wary of venturing from the compound and running into a hostile local who would shiv me a third eye, while Charlotte looked up old acquaintances and visited beaches I took to staying home to look after her cousins: twins, girls, seven years old, and the only people in town I could conceivably beat in an arm-wrestle.

I could also beat them at hide-and-seek, and at racing laps of the pool, and even at football. My drop kick sailed effortlessly past their guard and tumbled across the lawn to land in a gully where the garden ended and the rainforest began.

I was trotting after the ball to retrieve it when one of the girls tugged on my sleeve. 'You can't go down there; it isn't safe. The salties will munch you right up.'

'Salty' is, of course, a diminutive for saltwater crocodile, the 7-metre-long monster-lizard native to the tropics. I laughed, shook off the toddler, and jumped into the gully to retrieve the ball, misjudging the depth of the pool of still water and immediately sinking to my waist in mangrove swamp—the sort of ditch that salties live in. After a real adult had been summoned to fish me out, I was banned from playing outside, and for the rest of the trip I mainly hung out with Rocket, which was fine by me.

Rocket was the family cat, Charlotte's much-loved childhood pet, bought as a kitten and for solace as her parents broke up, in the hopes of purrs drowning out the fighting. I loved Rocket like I love all cats—immediately, irrationally. I'd been fond of cats my whole life, partially because of childhood loneliness alleviated by cuddles from my own cat and partially because of the brain parasite he gave me that now controls my thoughts.

Toxoplasma gondii is a parasitic protozoan that infects the human brain after transmission from cats. It's fairly harmless physically, although it can trigger severe mental disturbances in some people. Interestingly, these changes differ by gender—they make men more irrational, suspicious and jealous but tend to make women more warm-hearted, conscientious and kind.

It's worth noting that Charlotte and I probably both carry the parasite—me practically from birth, Charlotte from her childhood spent cuddling Rocket. It might explain the convergent paths our affections were taking the more time we spent together.

I don't know how Rocket felt about me, if she felt anything. Cats don't really give a shit. A cat barely cares if you live or die. They are not our pets, not really. They simply started hanging around to eat the rats that infested our silos about the time we developed agriculture. Cats are reticent when it comes to domesticity—in fact, they have barely been domesticated at all. While over the centuries we've bred dogs to work at a million precise tasks, cats have remained largely unchanged. If you go back a few millennia and look at the wall of a pyramid, you'll find a hieroglyphic cat identical to Rocket just sitting there, not giving a shit. Their one evolutionary concession to cohabitation with humans is that they've started meowing, a sound that triggers a protective instinct in the human subconscious. A cat is not my friend. It's a tiny, furry overlord who has infected me with a mind-controlling parasite so I'll feed it biscuits.

If Rocket wanted biscuits, I gave them to her. If Rocket wanted anything, I would do it. She was supposed to stay in after dark, but each night I let her out when she pleaded at the door, and on her return I would be rewarded with affectionate headbutts and sometimes the gift of a half-dead creature from the rainforest.

While I was getting along fine with Rocket, the rest of the family was yet to warm to me, the tiny, twitchy southerner with the brain parasite who spent all his days inside. Even Charlotte's boundless enthusiasm had plateaued as she began to realise that my passive aggression and propensity for cheap shots were perhaps not bandages over a bruised but golden heart, and, worse, that I would never make up for the missing love of an absent father.

So, in the evenings, shy in the company of the rest of the family, I drank too much. One evening, walking outside after too many beers, I stepped on something soft and smooth. In the dark, I leaned down and reached out a hand to identify the object under my fingers. It felt very much like a Glomesh purse my grandma had when I was young. I ran my hand along a good metre, perhaps a quarter of the length of the thing, before I realised I was stroking a python.

Of all the stupid traits humans have, anthropomorphism is among the silliest. It's the height of foolishness to ascribe our motivations to creatures that are physiologically fundamentally different from us. When the python turned lazily and fixed a glassy eye on me, and flicked its tongue over my leg once or twice, I read it as sinister, but who knows? I doubt a snake will ever understand how it feels to realise you are groping an apex predator, just like I will never understand how the world is rendered on the chemical sensory wonderland of the snake's tongue. The existential distance is too vast.

'Snake!' I yelled, or rather yelped, or meowed, perhaps, in a manner not entirely masculine, but one I hoped would trigger a protective instinct somewhere and summon someone to help me. '*Snake!*'

Charlotte's mum got to her feet, chuckling. 'Poor city boy,' she chided gently. 'Probably stepped on the hose.'

The party followed me out, jibing and japing, and, one by one, fell silent as the light of a dozen cell phones lit up the snake, and the bulge of a slowly digesting meal in its centre.

'It's good that he'd just eaten,' the snake handler told me shortly afterwards, 'otherwise, when you stepped on him he would have given you a goodnight hug and a half.'

This is a town where you can't get a pizza after 8 p.m., but in which you can summon a snake handler at midnight and fifteen minutes later his Hyundai Getz will trundle up the driveway.

Under the light of the snake handler's torch, we examined the creature. Its tongue flicked the air sleepily, as the football-sized bulge inched tailward.

'Yep,' said the snake handler, whistling low. 'Reckon that's a cat in there.'

There was a moment of silence, in which my heart plummeted, and it was met by a rising wail from Charlotte's mother: 'Rocket!'

The snake handler glanced over at her, shifted his bulk, tugged his T-shirt down over his gut, and said, with great sympathy, 'Sorry about that. I'll get him back for ya.'

'Will she be okay?' Charlotte's mum asked.

The handler didn't answer, but picked the snake up and shook it gently, to which it responded by vomiting up Rocket, half-digested, her fur patched and matted with digestive juices, her bones crushed.

Rocket was not okay. Nor was my relationship with Charlotte. It's hard to bounce back from accidentally feeding the brightest symbol of your partner's childhood to a snake.

Was any of this my fault, though? Would I have given in to Rocket and let her outside to her horrible death if her predecessors hadn't made me their brain-damaged manservant? My free will was mortgaged by the microscopic beast in my brain, and the purring one who brought me dead birds.

We are all slaves to instinct, some primordial rumbling in the genes. The cat needed to hunt, I needed to please the cat, and the snake needed to eat. A celestial game of rock-paper-scissors.

Depending on how you look at it, I am the rube in this play, or the victim, or the parasite, or the snake. I've never been able to figure out which, and I was never able to convince Charlotte to take comfort from the symbolism; from the fact that, while the story ended badly for Rocket, at least it ended, a nice clean break with a beginning, middle and end, and that, at least, was something I knew how to give her.

Lucky

Frank Robson

There is a space on the floor next to my desk where a dog used to be. He was a hellfire little terrier called Lucky, and when he died in November the space beside my desk seemed to leak its emptiness through the house and out into the streets and parks of the suburb where we lived. So my partner, Leisa, and I rented the house out and moved to another part of Brisbane. But, of course, the space moved with us.

It is there every morning when Lucky doesn't clamber up the bed to touch his nose to ours; it's there when his mortal enemies (cats, edge trimmers, lawnmowers, motorbikes, puffer fish) are allowed to go about their evil ways unmolested; it's the small fluffy ghosts that pass the corners of the eye; the phantom tactility of something warm and soft upon your palm, or pressed in sleep against your leg.

Lucky weighed just 8 kilograms, yet the void he left feels bottomless and permanent. He came to us by accident and ended up in a sort of experiment: could a ruffian mutt, ill-treated and then abandoned, develop (without discipline-based training) the sort of love and communication that crosses the species barrier? Could he become, of his own free will, not a segregated 'pet' but a full-time, reasonably behaved companion from an alternative gene pool?

Not, we soon discovered, without a lot of time and patience. Lucky was near death from a paralysing tick when his former owners left him at a veterinary clinic north of Brisbane and never returned. His matted fur was so overgrown he could barely see, but when the vet and his assistant had nursed him back to health, Lucky showed his inner lion: hurling himself at larger dogs during feeding to get his share. This was a foundling who'd had to fight for his supper.

Leisa and I heard about his plight in 2000, when he'd already spent three months living with the vet's assistant and was about to be euthanised for want of a new owner. So we drove to the clinic and brought him home. He was short, with stumpy legs, a tail that curled into a rigid circle, floppy ears and circular brown eyes that—despite his recent torments—met ours and held them unwaveringly.

Lucky turned out to be a canine eccentric. He could climb trees (grasping the trunk with his 'cabriolet' legs), piddle into the sea from the edge of our pitching yacht, and communicate via a twelve-snort vocabulary. He had a pathological loathing for cats and the sort of small, farty motors used in garden tools, but the real problem was that whenever we tried to put him on a leash he would turn and trot away.

Not just temporarily. Lucky was leaving forever, and would have done so a number of times if we hadn't run after him, or got the car and intercepted him blocks away. It was his leash phobia (probably a consequence of being tied up and left in misery) that led to our experiment. Because he was so smart and interested in everything, we opted not to subject him to choke chains and discipline-based training, but to try to win him over somehow. Through trust and friendship, we told ourselves, without much hope.

But after about two years, it had worked. Lucky sailed with us, dined with us at pavement cafes, attended our friends' parties, rode in the car while draped like a stole around one of our necks, slept on the end of our bed and spent his days on a cushion beside my home-office desk. He became one of the gang.

He responded by introducing us (through his looks, jokes, snorts and joyful affection) to the real him, and to depths of understanding with an animal we'd never experienced. Lucky stopped running away, accepted the leash and became—as a mate noted—'the happiest dog in the world'.

Then the three of us took off on a live-aboard sailing adventure that lasted almost three years, and the relationship became even closer. Always at our side, Lucky crept through spooky rainforests, explored deserted islands, clung stoically to his sofa during rough seas and hopped onto the chart table to oversee planning for each new leg of the journey. When we came home, I missed the sea and felt gloomy for months. But Lucky didn't care, because he was with us.

And then, about the start of last year, he began to fall behind on walks. Sometimes, if touched around the neck or shoulders, he'd flinch and growl. We thought it was arthritis, but an MRI scan revealed a large, inoperable tumour plaited through his upper spine. He was dying.

While he slept, dosed up with painkillers, Leisa and I wept and snivelled—victims, we began to realise, of our own curiosity about the extent of love and understanding possible between people and dogs. Of course it was Lucky, being impossible not to love, who dictated the outcome. And it was Lucky, with one of those grimly eloquent looks often recalled by dog lovers, who told us when it was time for him to go.

He couldn't stand by then, yet each morning when I went to my office he would give one of his famous snorts, summoning me to carry him to his spot beside my desk. On his last morning we carried him instead to the backyard, and lay with him on a quilt under the trees, waiting for the vet to come with his bright green injection.

Lucky's eyes closed calmly after the shot. 'He's gone,' said the vet. And he was. Completely gone.

Leaving only space.

Kid on a Crock

Andrew Rule

Melbourne Cup day 1948. A one-horse town called Birchip drowses in the Mallee heat. It's a day's journey by train and a world away from morning suits and manicured lawns at Flemington. George Neville, battler, is leaning on the bar at the Commercial Hotel. Like most of Australia, he and his mates are listening to the races on 'the wireless'.

George is a bow-legged bush jockey who once went around in a Caulfield Cup in the 1920s before coming home to Birchip. Feeds a couple of slow gallopers and thirteen kids the best he can.

Cut to Flemington. The track looks magnificent but beneath the turf it is soggy after days of rain. An obscure jumper called Finentigue has pinched the Cup Hurdle at 100-1. An omen, maybe, that it's a day for outsiders.

In the Cup, the interest is in the topweight, Howe, at 7-4 the hottest favourite since Phar Lap in 1930. The champion Harold Badger is on him, and they pulled a crowd of 101 000.

The odds say Howe has the Cup in the bag, but as the caller ticks off the rest of the field, back in Birchip George Neville automatically listens. All the way through the card to number 25, an 80-1 shot.

'Rimfire, R Neville, seven stone two,' the caller says.

George nearly drops his beer. 'R Neville' is his son, Ray—a tiny fifteen year old who's had nine race rides since getting his licence two months earlier.

George bolts for home. He calls in at the school, yelling to several of his offspring in the playground that their brother is riding in the Cup. The boldest of the Nevilles immediately wags school, heading to a cafe where there's a radio.

At home, George blurts the news. His wife is stunned. Why would anyone put a raw kid on a Melbourne Cup horse? She grabs her purse.

Flashback to the previous year. Little Ray is working on farms—driving tractors, trapping rabbits, plucking wool from dead sheep—but dreams of being a jockey. He gets his chance when an old local horseman recommends him to a respected Mordialloc trainer, Lou Robertson.

Ray and his suitcase catch the train to the city. His mother doesn't want him to go, but there are too many mouths to feed at home. He starts riding work as soon as he gets to Robertson's stables but doesn't get his race permit until the following season, just two months before the Cup carnival.

By that time Robertson has polished the boy's style. His first race ride is in a field of forty, up the straight six at Flemington. Two hours later, he wins the last race of the day on a stayer called Lincoln.

Cut to Cup eve. Rimfire, a handsome 6-year-old chestnut gelding with legs as patchy as his form, is still sore after finishing behind Howe in the Hotham Handicap. Rimfire is well named and well bred, grandson of the legendary Carbine, but so unsound that the people who leased him as a young horse have declined to pay the asking price of £2000 and sent him home to his breeder.

A leading lightweight jockey, WA Smith, has the Cup ride, but tells Rimfire's trainer, Stan Boydon, he'd rather ride Sun Blast because it is not so likely to break down.

With the clock ticking, Rimfire's connections need another lightweight. Why pick Neville? One story is that a stablehand suggests the boy from Birchip because of his win on Lincoln.

Rimfire's trainer books the ride with the boy's master. But the shrewd Robertson doesn't tell Neville until the next morning, making sure he sleeps soundly and has no time to be nervous.

Cup morning. Neville is up before dawn to ride work as usual. As he comes off the track, Robertson breaks the news.

'Hurry up and clean your gear,' he says. 'You're on Rimfire in the Cup.' As soon as the trainer is out of earshot, the stable foreman scoffs at Neville, 'If that bastard Rimfire wins, I'll walk from here to Sydney—barefoot.'

Public and the bookies agree. Rimfire is 80-1 and friendless. He has won only five races in four years, only once as favourite.

In the rooms, older jockeys laugh when the kid puts on Rimfire's colours. The jacket is so big the sleeves have to be rolled up and pinned; the tail reaches his knees before he tucks it into his breeches.

Neville borrows a lead bag from Smith, the rider who has turned down the Rimfire ride. Smith says, 'He'll be a good ride for you.' The kid asks innocently, 'Has he got a chance?', and Smith laughs.

'No, but he'll give you good experience.' He's right.

In the mounting yard, Rimfire looks good—for a crock that has limped off the track on three legs at his most recent win, months earlier, and pulled up sore after the Hotham Handicap three days earlier. His trainer has been putting cold compresses on the horse's legs until late the night before, hoping the authorities will let the horse run.

The sight of the baby-faced boy perched on Rimfire doesn't inspire confidence. The field includes some of Australia's best horses and some of the world's best jockeys: Williamson and Badger, Cook and Hutchinson, Thompson and Moore. From barrier 23, the kid eases the flashy chestnut crock across well behind the leaders, to be almost midfield passing the post the first time. Rimfire gradually gains ground, the kid sitting quietly as a bolter hares along in front. At the turn, as the leaders tire, Rimfire moves up to seventh place. Photographers snap the kid still sitting tight.

Then it happens. Rimfire forgets he is a cripple looking for a place to break down, and sweeps to the front ... just as the favourite, Howe, falters in his run with an injured ligament.

If it were a film, this is the moment when the audience starts cheering the underdog. In the real world, punters aren't so generous when longshots flog favourites.

Rimfire hits the front as Howe flounders. But the script calls for a tight finish. The Sydney Cup winner Dark Marne, ridden by the ice-cold Sydney jockey Jack Thompson, sets out after Rimfire. Thompson pulls the whip and lifts his horse closer with every stride. His horse is on the rails, the kid's is on the ropes. They hit the line locked together ... the favourite and the joker in the pack.

Afterwards, the boy tells reporters: 'I was so excited halfway down the straight at the thought of winning the Melbourne Cup that I hardly realised Dark Marne was so close.'

The taciturn Thompson thinks he's won. So certain he wheels his horse around first and trots back in front, tells waiting reporters he's got the money. One of the other senior riders calls to Neville: 'Do you reckon you got there, son?'

'Well, I hope I did,' the boy replies doubtfully. A sea of punters hope he's wrong. He rides back to scale in front of a hushed crowd.

For the first time in Cup history, the judge calls for a photograph from the new finish camera: it shows Rimfire by a nostril.

Angry punters boo. Thompson, the hard man who is to ride for another thirty-five years, swears to the day he dies that the camera was faulty, and that Dark Marne won.

Meanwhile, in Birchip, Neville's parents run to the hotel in time for the race. His mother has 'a quid' each way with the SP bookmaker in the bar.

One of the Neville brothers sneaks back to school after the race and is caught by the teacher, who produces a strap. Luckily, he asks what won the Cup. When the boy says, 'Me brother did, sir,' the teacher lets him off—and declares a half-holiday for the school. It's a big day in Birchip.

Late that afternoon, the kid goes back to Mordialloc in the horse float, clutching 'twenty-five quid' Rimfire's owner has given him. He gets an extra-large serve of steak and eggs to celebrate, and is allowed to go to Wirth's Circus to be presented with a trophy whip.

Next day is his sixteenth birthday. He's up at 4 a.m. to ride work and muck out stables. The fairy story's over. Fade to black …

············

The boy from Birchip turned sixty-four just before Bart Cummings won his tenth Cup, with Saintly in 1996. Exactly forty-eight years after he piloted Rimfire into Melbourne Cup folklore, it's hard to tell whether grandfather Neville is tired of recalling his brush with the big time, or just modest. Maybe both.

It's true that the chapter of Ray Neville's life that reads like a film script closed on that golden afternoon in 1948. But, in his own way, he has lived happily ever after.

He didn't go on to a glorious career in the saddle. But he didn't vanish without riding another winner, either, contrary to myth.

The truth is somewhere in between. Like many apprentices, Neville got heavy. He won a few more times, but within eighteen months of the Cup couldn't make the tiny weights he needed to ride in claiming races.

Too big to be an apprentice jockey, he became a small apprentice carpenter. At first, he worked in Melbourne but he soon went back to the bush. And stayed there. But he didn't stay out of the saddle.

As a schoolboy, he had loved riding over jumps at local shows. He'd listened to the stories of the old 'jumping men' his father knew. It wasn't long before the only carpenter ever to win a Melbourne Cup dusted off his childhood ambitions and dreamed of adding the Grand National steeplechase to his record.

He'd been 'riding work' for trainers around Birchip, and taking the occasional flat ride at country meetings. One day an old jumps trainer, Reuben Fisher, asked him if he wanted to ride in a hurdle race.

'Yeah,' Neville replied.

'Ever done it before?'

'No,' said Neville.

'Well, you're the right man for the job,' said the old timer drily. 'Because the horse has never been over jumps either.' The horse ran second. Neville was hooked.

For nearly twenty years he built houses Monday to Friday, schooling jumpers before work. Saturdays he rode in races for 'three quid' a losing ride, more for the occasional winner.

It helped feed the kids. He had eight.

His biggest win was the Commonwealth Steeplechase. He didn't win a National. The closest he came in Warrnambool's famous Grand Annual was fourth. But he won plenty of other races, including a few for the premier, Sir Henry Bolte.

He was stable jockey for a Mallee trainer, Reg Fisher. When Fisher moved from Rainbow to Stawell in 1966, the Nevilles went with him—and stayed.

Neville's second racing career ended in a Ballarat steeplechase in 1969, when his horse fell and crushed him.

'I woke up next morning in St John's Hospital with one arm in plaster and one leg in plaster and said, "That's it. I've given it away." I came right six months later, but I couldn't go back on my word.' As soon as he was fit enough, he started riding work again. He kept it up until he turned sixty. After that he still got up at dawn to help his eldest son, Geoff, a former rodeo rider, who broke in young horses for other trainers.

Jumping jockeys are a tough breed. Like a lot of the cross-country fraternity, Neville looks a bit like an old fighter because he was one. A nugget of a man, with square hands, a strong jaw, a gruff manner and the sort of neatly parted hair that used to be seen in Brylcreem ads.

A blue singlet shows up beneath a well-filled check shirt. He'd tip the scales at nearly double the featherweight he was in 1948.

There are two big photographs on the mantelpiece. One, a striking picture of Rimfire with the teenage Neville in the saddle. The other, in an oval frame, of the Nevilles' wedding in 1955. June Neville was a Mallee bride, born and bred at Beulah.

'Isn't everybody sick of this story?' Neville grumbles.

But he doesn't protest as June proudly produces each piece of Melbourne Cup memorabilia. Here's a copy of the Cup trophy, presented by the GMH car company. The plating is tarnished. 'It's gone a bit black from the gas fire,' June says apologetically.

And there's the gold-mounted whip presented by Wirth's Circus to the winning jockey. It lives on the mantelpiece next to the Rimfire photograph.

Then June produces a miniature set of Rimfire's colours—white, light blue sleeves and red cap—that she ran up herself on the sewing machine. The grandkids love them, she says, eyes shining.

Finally, she produces a recent snapshot of her husband in a jacket and tie, and tells the story that goes with it.

The previous year, the Birchip Shire went out of existence because it was amalgamated with others into the Buloke Shire. It decided to mark the occasion by honouring Birchip's most famous sons.

One was the country singer Dusty Rankin, who made his first record in 1948. The other was Ray.

'Yeah,' he cut in. 'The old bloke that rang said they usually wait until you die, but this time they decided to do it while we were still alive.'

So he and June put on their Sunday best and drove up to Birchip for the function.

After the speeches Ray was asked to pull back a tiny curtain. Behind it was a metal plaque of a jockey boy on a racehorse.

Ray Neville died in 2008.

Animal Acts

John Silvester

The private schoolboy was beginning to doubt the wisdom of choosing former standover man Mark 'Chopper' Read as the subject of a short documentary that was part of his senior-year assessment.

As he sat on the couch next to Read, ready to film an interview, Chopper's dog, Kayser (named after his defence lawyer, Boris Kayser), placed his fearsome snout uncomfortably close to the young man's lap.

'What's the matter?' asked Read. 'Haven't you ever sat with someone with no ears, with a dog about 2 inches from your knackers?'

It was a rhetorical question. While both Read and Kayser looked ferocious, their days of crime were behind them.

Read wasn't one to bear a grudge. He once named a grey-hound 'The Buggster' after Tasmania's then Director of Public Prosecutions, Damian Bugg QC, who had sent the self-confessed killer to jail for an indefinite sentence. The greyhound was slower than Australia Post but the barrister was fast-tracked to become Commonwealth DPP and Chancellor of the University of Tasmania.

When finally released, Read moved to a Tasmanian farm with two terriers, Reggie and Ronnie, named after London's criminal Kray brothers. Sadly, the terriers had the same bloodthirsty streak as their namesakes and had to be put down for killing chickens.

Not that Read was always a committed animal lover. He once admitted to killing an enemy's small dog, barbecuing it with garlic salt and making the rival eat his former pet accompanied only with American mustard.

Crooks are often referred to as animals (dogs, jackals, hyenas, rats, maggots and stool pigeons), which is wildly unfair to the non-human community. In fact, many colourful characters have an affinity for pets—often based on companionship but some-times for practical purposes.

Prolific drug dealer and killer Dennis Allen kept attack geese at his Richmond house, believing they were more effective than guard dogs. As he dealt in cash, had more jewellery than Elizabeth Taylor and was a prodigious police informer, the watchful geese were a wise investment.

One of Allen's relatives also had an interest in birds, of the canary variety, until her favourite went missing during a police raid. She concluded that a detective (who himself had a wildlife nickname) had freed the feathered pet in an act of petulance. That is, until she opened the freezer to find the bird wedged between the fish fingers and the raspberry ripple, extremely dead.

Master armed robber and alleged gangland killer Russell Cox didn't stay on the run for eleven years after escaping from Sydney's maximum-security Katingal jail division by taking risks.

He was a master of disguise, with a number of aliases, including 'Mr Walker' from the *Phantom* comics. Even his dog, Devil, had a fake name, answering to Butch. 'Mr Walker' and 'Butch' went for early-morning runs because Cox liked to be out of the house by sunrise, knowing that police preferred to conduct raids at dawn.

Hitman and former poodle breeder James Frederick Bazley had great affection for dogs but little time for victims. Bazley was paid $20 000 to murder drug couriers Isabel and Douglas Wilson, whose bodies were found buried in Rye in May 1979. The Wilsons were killed on the orders of the Mr Asia drug syndicate boss, Terrance John Clark, after corrupt police confirmed the couple were talking to Queensland detectives.

The hitman was instructed to kill the Wilsons' dog, Taj, and drop the victims' car at Melbourne airport to give the impression they had fled overseas. He parked the car as ordered but refused to kill the dog, instead dropping it in the street on his way through Brunswick.

Another gangster with a weakness for little dogs was Mario Condello, a qualified lawyer who once had ambitions to be a High Court judge and a tooled-up mobster but ended up as a mobbed-up tool.

The big man liked to take his dog for an early-morning walk, always using the same route past the Brighton cemetery. For a fellow connected with the so-called Carlton Crew and up to his armpits in the Melbourne gangland war, such predictability could be fatal. Sure enough, in 2004 a police taskforce found that drug boss Carl Williams had put out a contract to kill Condello on his morning walk.

On the day, police made sure Condello was nowhere near Brighton as the two-man hit team assembled. In a sliding-doors moment, another large local with a small dog walked past the cemetery, leading the would-be killers to think they had their man.

A police bug picked up one crook saying, 'I'm going to have to walk up beside him and shoot him.'

As there were 170 police hiding in the area, the gunmen were quickly arrested before they could move. Worried detectives were instantly relieved, as was the bladder of one of the gunmen. We will never know if the wrong man discovered how close he was to becoming a mistaken-identity victim.

Condello was safe for a time but continued to be a creature of habit. Given bail on the condition he spent nights at home, he fell into a routine of returning there around the same time. He was shot dead two years later, in his driveway. The suspect in this case disliked most people and preferred the company of a parrot he taught to say 'Not guilty' and 'I hate coppers'. Who says stone killers don't have a sense of humour?

It is not only the baddies who have affection for animals. Police dogs have a wonderful history of catching crooks and protecting their handlers, something bent drug squad cop David Miechel forgot when caught outside an East Oakleigh drug house he happened to be robbing.

Found up a tree by a canine unit, Miechel first tried to talk his way out, saying he was looking for the offender. When that failed, he punched the handler, which enraged police dog Silky, who proceeded to latch onto his thigh.

Miechel then tried to punch the dog, which enraged the handler, who hit him with a police torch, fracturing his cheekbone and jaw. Miechel got a nasty scar and twelve years, while Silky got a plate of Meaty Bites.

Miechel's co-offender Terence Hodson made a statement implicating then detective sergeant Paul Dale but did not live to testify. In May 2004 Hodson and his wife Christine were shot dead in their Kew home. Their two guard dogs were locked in the garage, suggesting the victims did not feel threatened and were ambushed by someone they knew. Had the dogs been left out, it might have saved the Hodsons.

For a time the elite Purana police taskforce had its own office pet—a mature-age yabby found in a Castlemaine dam and kept in a 25-litre glass receptacle previously used to produce amphetamines.

The container was seized from a lab owned by drug boss Tony Mokbel, and so the freshwater crustacean was named Tony. Both yabby Tony and runaway Tony seemed to like boats. The drug boss escaped to Greece in a $340 000 ketch, while the yabby had a $2 toy one at the bottom of the tank.

Eventually, administrative staff bought a goldfish dubbed Zarah (after lawyer Zarah Garde-Wilson, who, incidentally, owned a snake called Chivas) but the yabby ate the fish, proving that Tony neither could be trusted nor was fond of captivity.

This brings us to one of the great criminological and zoological mysteries of our time—the unexplained death of Australia's oldest armed robber, Aubrey Maurice Broughill. When, in February 1999, Aubrey's body was found floating in a flooded Wodonga quarry, his death was treated as suspicious.

There was no reason for him to be there. He had no car. There was no record he travelled to the district on public transport, and accommodation checks showed no bookings for him. He was seventy-three years old but fit and a strong swimmer.

When the body was recovered, he was wearing a striped shirt, his blue denim jeans were caught around his left foot, his belt was still fastened, he was not wearing underpants and he was barefoot.

There was another reason to think this was no accident. Aubrey Maurice Broughill had no testicles.

One theory put to the coroner was that the local population of eastern snake-necked turtles—which usually snack on insects, small fish, tadpoles and the occasional frog—attacked him after death.

While the snake-necked turtle is known to be partial to carrion, no one can explain why in this case it supposedly went after only one part of the anatomy. When these turtles find a carcass they use their front claws to shred the flesh into bite-size chunks.

Which seems at odds with the description of Broughill's injuries as a 'well-defined incised like edge measuring seven centimetres and extending to a more irregular ragged tear'. This would suggest that, unless the turtles were armed with scalpels, they are not guilty.

Broughill had teamed up with some South Australian thieves, and had been charged with nineteen offences, including burglary and car theft, just weeks earlier. Adelaide police had connected this gang to the mysterious disappearance of four men over a seven-year period. Their bodies have not been found.

If you lie down with dogs, fleas are the least of your problems.

Mimi and Rosa

Jeff Sparrow

I bestow on you the highest honour I can award a mortal being; I shall entrust you my Mimi. [... Y]ou'll have to abduct her in the car in your arms (definitely not in a basket or a sack!!!) with the help of my housekeeper ... she will pack all Mimi's seven belongings (her little box, cat litter, bowl, cushions and—please—a red armchair which she is used to).

The instructions might have been written by any contemporary cat lover—perhaps someone embarking on a vacation and carefully instructing a friend on how to care for their precious animal. Actually, though, they're from the great German socialist Rosa Luxemburg, written as she prepared for jail, a few years before her murder.

Companion animals—especially cats—can have that effect. They strip away the years. One cat lover recognises another, no matter the temporal divide separating them.

> Yesterday evening this is what [Mimi] did. I was searching all the rooms for her, but she wasn't there. I was getting worried, and I then discovered her in my bed, but she was lying so that the cover was tucked up prettily right under her chin with her head on the pillow exactly the way I lie, and she looked at me calmly and roguishly.

Add a photo, and the extract from a 1908 letter by Luxemburg could be a Facebook post popping up on your feed today. Perhaps, then, Mimi can help recover her owner from a hundred years of history—and the various mythologies that have claimed her.

Luxemburg was born into a Jewish family in an anti-Semitic Poland in 1871. A socialist from her teens, she fled to Zurich, where she earned her PhD. Eventually, she made her way to Berlin, to become a major activist, theorist and orator in the Social Democratic Party, the largest socialist organisation in Europe.

Upon the outbreak of the Great War, almost all the leading German socialists embraced the kaiser's military effort. Luxemburg's refusal to capitulate to the war hysteria made her, with her comrade Karl Liebknecht, a worldwide symbol of revolutionary intransigence.

After the insurrection that brought the conflict to an end, the pair died at the hands of soldiers from the *freikorps* (precursors to the Nazis). Thereafter, German conservatives remembered Luxemburg as the terrifying Red Rosa, a sinister Tricoteuse fomenting bloody revolt, while the East German ideologues celebrated her as a stern communist saint.

It's difficult to imagine either version of Luxemburg fussing over exactly how a cat should be transported.

Mimi carried in a basket, taken for a day and then brought back! As if it was a question of an ordinary creature of the species *felix domestic*. Well, you should know ... that Mimi is a little mimosa, a hyper nervous little princess in cat's fur and when I, her own mother, once wanted to carry her out of the house against her will, she got cramp due to the excitement and turned stiff in my arms so that she had to be brought back into the apartment with distressed little eyes and only recovered after some hours. Yes, yes, you have no idea what my motherly heart has already experienced.

Of course, the instant familiarity of the passage can produce a different kind of historical disorientation. We might even say that the gradual awareness of Luxemburg's letters—published in dribs and drabs since the 1920s and recently compiled in a wonderful collection by Verso—spawned a new myth, one in which Mimi plays a starring role.

For instance, in her book *The Demon Lover*, the radical feminist Robin Morgan depicts Luxemburg as torn 'between a relentless political activism and her yearning for a contemplative life of writing, thinking and caring for plants and animals'. This (surprisingly common) perception of Luxemburg as an almost Tolstoyian pacifist awkwardly shoehorned into the socialist movement comes, in part, from the devotion to Mimi chronicled in Luxemburg's prodigious correspondence to friends and comrades.

We read of the cat's misbehaviour ('Mimi is a scoundrel. She leaped at me from the floor and tried to bite me') and the cat's affection ('Mimi showed she was happy with me right away and has again become high-spirited, comes running to me like a dog and grabs at the train of my dress'). She bites the nose of a marble bust and she chases the light refracted from a prism ('Soon she deduced that there was "nothing" to them, that they were just an optical illusion, and then she would watch the dance with her merry little eyes, without bestirring herself'). She helps her owner spray flowers; she reads a letter by 'sniff[ing] at it lovingly'.

'Mimi is loved by all,' Luxemburg boasts in 1911, 'and today in the presence of the Adolf [Warski] family she caused universal amazement, because she was standing on two paws, holding onto the water faucet and with one paw catching the falling drips and accompanying them on their downward course.'

Alongside pride in Mimi's accomplishments (again, so very familiar from social media), Luxemburg's letters do, sometimes, voice her utter exhaustion, her desire to escape the whirlwind of activism, 'to paint and live on a little plot of land where I can feed and love the animals'.

'How glad I am,' she writes, 'that three years ago I suddenly plunged into the study of botany the way I do everything, immediately, with all my fire and passion, with my entire being, so that the world, the party, and my work faded away for me and only one passion filled me up both day and night: to be outdoors roaming about in the springtime fields, to gather plants until my arms were full, and then at home to put them in order, identify them, and put them between the pages of a scrapbook to dry.'

When, on another occasion, a fellow socialist describes a starving worker staring hungrily at meat bought for Mimi, Luxemburg snaps back: 'Why are you telling me this? Don't I do everything in my power to fight for all the poor? You shouldn't spoil my joy with Mimi.'

Yet, if Mimi represents for Luxemburg a refuge from political turmoil, the cat is also, without question, a companion within it. Luxemburg discovered the injured animal at the SPD school where she taught political economy—and her relationship with the cat unfolded more or less entirely within the well-organised world of the German labour movement.

'I should be working,' she writes in 1912, 'but I'm feeling lazy. Mimi is rolling over teasingly on the carpet, saying *prau* [meow] and letting herself be tickled on the tummy.'

That feline-assisted procrastination will strike a chord with any cat-owning writer today. But, precisely because of that, it's easy to forget that Luxemburg's 'work' was that of a professional revolutionary in the midst of world-shaking events.

Furthermore, if she discusses the stresses of her public life, she also explains the satisfaction politics provides her. She describes, for instance, the period she spent writing her magnum opus, *The Accumulation of Capital*, as the happiest time of her life—a happiness she shares with Mimi.

'Really,' she recalls, 'I was living as though in euphoria, "on a high", say and heard nothing else, day or night, but this one question which unfolded before me so beautifully, and I don't know what to say about which gave me the greater pleasure: the process of thinking, when I was turning a complicated problem over in my mind, pacing slowly back and forth through the room, under the close and attentive observation of Mimi who lay on the red plush tablecloth with her little paws curled under her and kept turning her wise head back and forth to follow my movements; or the process of giving shape and literary form to my thoughts with pen in hand.'

It's a passage that inspires Kate Evans (in her terrific graphic novel *Red Rosa*) to depict Luxemburg expounding her theory of imperialism to a scowling Comrade Mimi.

The cat is also present in 1911 when Luxemburg meets with Lenin. 'I enjoy talking with him,' she writes later, 'he's clever and well educated, and has such an ugly mug, the kind I like to look at.' Naturally, she also claims that Mimi impresses Lenin 'tremendously':

> He said that only in Siberia had he seen such a magnificent creature, that she was a *baskii kot*—a majestic cat. She also flirted with him, rolled on her back and behaved enticingly toward him, but when he tried to approach her she whacked him with a paw and snarled like a tiger.

(Lenin's own affection for cats would require an entirely separate article.)

Luxemburg loved animals—and it's clear that she used Mimi to express different facets of her complex personality. Many of her references to the cat come in letters to her lovers, particularly Kostya Zetkin. 'I kiss you,' she writes, in a typical passage. 'Mimi does too.'

Yet, politically, she remained, as she said, 'as hard as polished steel'—even as she delighted in 'Mimi ... sleeping next to me on the easy chair, curled up like a snail.'

Hearing of Luxemburg's exhaustion, her friend (and sometime lover) Leo Jogiches commented: 'If Rosa lived differently, she would be even less satisfied. She cannot live differently.'

That seems entirely true.

In another letter to Kostya, she encloses 'as a gift a picture of Mimi, which I got yesterday and which gave me great joy'. That photograph, unfortunately, doesn't seem to have survived. In its absence, we can't say much about Mimi—her colour or breed or size. Nor is it clear what happened to the animal after Luxemburg's death.

With characteristic courage, Luxemburg accepted the danger she faced.

'I would not flee,' she told a friend at the start of the war, 'even if I were threatened by the gallows, and that is for the simple reason that I consider it absolutely necessary to accustom our party to the idea that sacrifices are part of a socialist's work in life, that they are simply a matter of course.'

After the failed uprising in 1918, the government (led by one of Luxemburg's former students) placed a price on her head. Soldiers, whipped up into an anti-Semitic frenzy by the right-wing press, arrested Luxemburg in an apartment on Mannheim Strasse and took her to their headquarters at the Hotel Eden. She walked through a crowd of uniformed men showering her with abuse. They clubbed her unconscious, shot her dead and dumped her body in the Spree river.

In the paragraph below she writes to her friend about her attitude to World War I—and, in the process, explains something of what the animal she calls 'my most blessed cat Mimi' meant to her. It seems, then, an appropriate epitaph, both for the cat and the woman who loved her.

'Don't you understand,' Luxemburg says, 'that the overall disaster is much *too great* to be moaned and groaned about? I can grieve or feel bad if Mimi is sick, or if you are not well. But when the whole world is out of joint, then I merely seek to understand what is going on and why, and then I have done my duty, and I am calm and in good spirits from then on. *Ultra posse nemo obligatur* [none are obliged to do more than they can]. And then for me there still remains everything else that makes me happy: music and painting and clouds and doing botany in the spring and good books and Mimi and you and much more.'

Roo Dogs

Paul Toohey

Tough guys like their pit bulls. But do they know there was a time when tough guys were really tough? They were explorers, hunters, pastoralists and hungry Aboriginal hinterland probers, forced off their country into the wastelands. All of them had only one kind of dog at their side: the kangaroo dog.

Until thirty years ago, it was still possible to see kangaroo dogs on some cattle stations and farms. They were tall, rangy and heavier-chested than a greyhound. Mean-looking. Some carried subtle tiger markings—hinting at both Tasmanian and Bengal varieties. You knew a kangaroo dog. They carried war scars from wildly scratching kangaroos.

And there always seemed to be two of them. They wouldn't vault and slaver, or necessarily bite. They'd sit back, frigidly observing through sideways eyes. Waiting to see what happened.

What happened was that our national dog, which long predated the blue heeler as the preferred canine sidekick, all but disappeared. Probably only a couple of hundred true-to-type kangaroo dogs still exist.

'They were once part of our history,' says James Callan, a hunting-dog breeder from Warren in central New South Wales, who has one young female kangaroo dog in his pack. But his family has had them for generations. 'They were the first type of dog to be developed in Australia.'

The kangaroo dog was not a breed but a type. It was basically a cross between a greyhound and a deerhound. The greyhound was fast and clever but its feet were too soft; crossed with a deerhound, it became tougher and had a better instinct for running off or killing the dingoes that circled the settlers' herds. The ideal kangaroo dog leaned towards the greyhound's short coat. Prickles didn't attach and it was low-maintenance.

The dog became a lifesaver for pioneers, whose weapons weren't always accurate over long ranges. With a kangaroo dog, no gun was needed. It could outpace and kill kangaroos, as Aborigines were quick to notice. They came to prefer them to their less reliable—and always self-interested—dingoes.

James Callan was driving through Coober Pedy several years ago at dusk when 'We saw some Aborigines walking along, followed by a big heap of their dogs. You could see those dogs still had a bit of roo dog in them, but nothing full'.

The kangaroo dog bounds through Australian history. Author James Boyce wrote that in the early 1800s, Tasmanian chaplain and diarist Robert Knopwood had roo dogs and was selling kangaroo meat and skins to the government. As Boyce put it: 'Dogs remained the key to the bushrangers' freedom, ensuring food, a source of cash, and warmth, and the capacity to obtain all these on the move. The most powerful bushranger to ever roam Van Diemen's Land, Michael Howe, was reported to have been loyal to only two objectives, and well chosen they were: his Aboriginal partner, Black Mary, and his kangaroo dog, Bosun.'

Ludwig Leichhardt relied on kangaroo dogs for his 1844–45 overland expedition. He told how 'most unfortunately our kangaroo dog had been left behind, whereby this most valuable animal was lost. He has been the means for obtaining so much, and indeed the greatest part of our game, that his loss was severely felt by us'.

Sydney ginger beer maker Nicodemus Dunn commissioned Thomas Balcombe to paint one of his favoured roo dogs, in 1853. At that time, 'formal' kangaroo hunts were the rage, as the local version of the fox hunt.

A British officer, Sir Samuel Baker, shipped kangaroo dogs to the subcontinent in the 1840s for his sambar deer, jackal and boar hunts. Of one animal, Lena, he said: 'She was an Australian bitch of great size, courage and beauty.'

But Baker really admired Killbuck, his male, telling how splendid it was 'to witness the bounding spring of Killbuck as he pinned an elk [sambar] at bay that no other dog could touch. He had a peculiar knack of seizing that I've never seen equalled. No matter what position the elk might be, he was sure to have him … it was certain death for the animal …'

A kangaroo dog was exhibited at the first international dog show in London, in 1863, winning a silver medal in the 'large foreign dogs' category. The Prince of Wales exhibited a pair of Australian-born and -bred kangaroo dogs the following year.

In 1914, Robert Kaleski compiled perhaps the first book describing dogs peculiar to Australia. 'The first [kangaroo] dogs were very big, bony devils, with a light coat of shaggy hair; game as bulldogs and fierce as tiger cats. They ran both by scent and sight; some, but not many, of the present dogs do the same. One of them was a match for any kangaroo or dingo that ever walked.'

South Australian sheep-station manager John McEntee recalled for an ABC history program how 'settlers brought in what we term kangaroo dogs. I don't know what was mixed with them but they're huge … as soon as the Aborigines saw these hounds that could keep up with the kangaroo and pull it down and there's your feed, they scrapped their dingoes.'

Then, quietly, the kangaroo dog slipped from view. It was partly because accurate rifles became commonplace. A rifle didn't need to be fed anything but a bullet. And it was more than that, as James Callan explains: 'The main thing is when the rabbit population exploded, people had what they called rabbit packs—huge packs of dogs, up to one hundred of them, run by a dogman. People would employ a dogman to get rid of rabbits. The dogman had kangaroo dogs, beagles, staghounds and sheep and cattle dogs. The smaller dogs would have been the scent hunters—they'd flush out the rabbits. The dogman would use the roo dogs to kill 'em.'

When myxomatosis was unleashed in 1950, the rabbit population plunged from 600 million to 100 million. Kangaroo dogs, by then rabbit dogs, were not needed. 'All these dogmen were stuck with these dogs,' says Callan. And the biggest, hungriest dogs were the first to go. 'They all got shot. There was no employment and no way of feeding them. That's where we lost most of them.

'And, by then, most of them were becoming mongrelised with the wider rabbit-pack breeds anyway. Only a few of the farmers that owned a couple of staghounds or kangaroo dogs kept 'em. And that's basically all what's left.'

So why not simply put a greyhound to a deerhound and start the type again? It's not, they say, that simple. You might get a dog that looks like a kangaroo dog, but it may be a shell of the real thing.

Callan cites the case of Rhodesian ridgebacks in Australia. 'With ridgebacks, they were a southern African farm, hunting and guard dog. When they first brought them over here, it was a really good hunting dog—it'd fetch ducks and game.' The dog lost those abilities, says Callan. It became valued for its appearance.

'That's what show judges are interested in. But the prettiest dog in the litter mightn't be the best worker.'

The inner mutt—the one with all the instinct and attitude, the true kangaroo dog or ridgeback of old—may fail the aesthetic test. It's like life itself. For every fifty decent, hard-working, rough-around-the-edges blokes there'll always be a Jamie Durie.

'I'm a member of the kennel club,' says Callan, referring to the national organisation that decides on 'standard' types. 'We're trying to think about getting them up and going again and getting them registered. But we don't know whether it's a good thing or a bad thing.' Callan doesn't want to see kangaroo dogs revived in the show circuit if all they are is backyard cat-chasers.

Kaleski wrote, in 1914: 'The price of a kangaroo dog is anything from one pound to 20 pounds, according to his sense and reputation. No money will buy a really wise one from a shooter because he could not do without him. Besides, after the cattle dog, he is the most useful dog in the bush—a grand mate, the best game dog, a great fighter and watchdog.'

Says Callan: 'We don't want the very few left being shown as a novelty and seeing the line ruined.' Callan and his friends, who hold in their dogs a direct line back to the first days of settlement, will have to make a call one way or the other.

Society of Birds

Don Watson

e.e. cummings prayed that his heart would always be open to little birds. My family, the maternal side especially, has always shared some of his sentiment. It goes back to the clearing of the forest. As the trees went, the little birds came and dwelled in the hydrangeas under the window. Fantails, wagtails, blue wrens, scrubwrens, honeyeaters, eastern rosellas, finches, silver-eyes, robins, thornbills, mudlarks and thrushes: generations of us have watched them from the kitchen and talked to them as if to friends or children. If it is one of the last pagan associations in what remains of the rural Protestant, or has a more philosophical origin, I do not know.

I do know that Cummings' line does not ring quite true. Birds are less a matter of the heart than of the senses. We are not talking about commitment, but rather the pleasure a bird's shape and sound afford us, and the wonder of its aeronautics. These things might be surrogates for something deeper (try holding a grey thrush in your hand and see if it doesn't stir something) but the first conscious sensations that birds create are aesthetic ones. A hovering kite, an egret by the water's edge, a thrush singing by the window—in every bird's construction there is first an irresistible line.

Consider that thrush. It is a very ordinary flyer, yet in appearance it is at least as pure a bird as the swallow: a swallow, in truth, is such an aerial acrobat as to seem part bat.

'Whatever the bird is, is perfect in the bird,' Judith Wright wrote. And no bird is quite as perfect as a thrush. In the same verse Wright also talks of parrots and kestrels, but I think it's a fair bet that a thrush—'round as a mother or a full drop of water'—inspired the line about perfection.

'Whatever the bird does is right for the bird to do,' Wright says, and contrasts that happy state with her own, which is 'torn and beleaguered'. It's a beautiful line, but like Cummings', as untrue as it is true.

This spring, whenever I opened the back door, a magpie took off from its nest in a gum tree half a kilometre away and came skimming over the grass, arcing over the fences, zooming beneath the branches down the drive and veering straight at my brow, before braking impossibly late and landing on the porch rail beside me. It all took about five seconds. I've no doubt the magpie was showing me how exhilarating flying is for the creatures that can do it. And then it carolled.

Another magpie, with a nest on a higher branch, always followed the first, but it did not fly with the same élan or straight at me, and it always pulled up a metre further away. It was a shyer bird and its carol was more guttural. The first took the meat from my hand, the second only when I put it down. Both flew straight back to their nests, fed their pleading young with my mince and came sailing back to the porch again.

The young have now left the nests. In the morning they follow their parents to my back porch and whine for food while the adults warble away in their mezzo-sopranos until I come out. No unprejudiced human being could fail to be improved by the presence of magpies. They are fearless, resourceful, amusing and melodious; and, above all—as all birds have to be—stoic. But they also contain complexities of character: not in the multitudes of some humans, perhaps, but not that many less than the average. And, just to go on the sample at my door, between one magpie and another there are differences as pronounced as they are between, say, the Three Tenors, or two modern political leaders when there is an election on.

Last week on a local road I saw a kookaburra dive from a fence post on one side to the verge of the other; in pursuit of what I don't know, because in the instant that it dived, a man on a motorbike roared round the corner and the bird's head struck the front wheel. The collision killed the kookaburra: it bounced back across the road and lay there on its back, quite still. What Australian does not love kookaburras? To be truthful, in that moment I would have been no more dismayed if it had been the motorcyclist on his back and the kookaburra flying on down the road.

What this bird did was *wrong* for the bird to do. Yet it was only a minor departure from the normal drama of bird life. Watch birds for a while, and you begin to see that what is natural for the bird is perpetual menace, frequent terror and sudden death—much of it inflicted by other birds—and to all this they must find solutions.

Around midnight a couple of nights ago, a honeyeater of some kind crashed into the wire-screen door and clung there shuddering. There was an owl in the trees outside. If owls are wise, it must be only in the daytime. When darkness falls they are ruthless, havoc-creating monsters. The owl and the pussycat went to sea, and when night fell the owl tore the cat to pieces.

Every day in the society of birds down by the lake, harriers, kites, falcons and eagles glide among their fellows, brazenly looking for one to kill. Patches of feathers and down on the ground—all-white, pink and grey, red and blue, green and yellow—are all they leave of any bird they catch, and the proof of their efficiency. They are the SS of the lake. Like owls, they use not just the weapon of surprise, but that of terror. They hunt in pairs or trios: hovering over the marshes on the edge, or sweeping and swerving low over the gums and willows in the hope that their sudden appearance, or the equally potent effect of their shadow, will frighten something out.

They glide and soar and dive in accordance with their natures and our ideal of them. But they also concoct, invent and improvise. On windy days they let the air carry them wildly from tree to tree, as if to use unruliness as a disguise and to heighten the terrible effect of their shadows.

At dusk, when flocks of galahs, corellas and cockatoos go screeching home, the hawks station themselves in trees, or glide and swirl about looking for their chance. But at the same time of the day, I have watched a falcon stand for twenty minutes in the reeds by the edge of the lake. I thought it was counting on ducks or cygnets coming ashore, but when a flock of parrots flew overhead the falcon climbed into the air—and into the parrots—like a surface-to-air missile. On another occasion, it hid for a long time in the grass on one side of a low ridge, then suddenly soared into the air and swooped down the other side and onto some creature it must have sensed was there.

In response to the raptors' ingenuity, the parrots have worked out their own defences, which amount to a kind of Resistance. They post evening lookouts in the trees and on the ground. They divide their flocks. They fly jagged, crazy paths. They communicate endlessly. No galah or cockatoo ever seems to move without screeching a message of some kind to every other galah or cockatoo within a kilometre, and none ever hears a screech without replying.

And they are served by other species: by the magpies and mudlarks that spend a good part of every day obeying their ferocious territorial instincts and driving raptors from their airspace, and by crows whose motives might be more subjective.

If there is one bird unloved even by those who love birds, it is a crow. (In fact they're ravens, but in the language they are crows.) Crows are hated because they are black and symbolise death and drought; because their cawing is maudlin and depressing; and because they are eaters of carrion. What is worse, they eat dying animals before they are dead. Unable to pierce the hide of feeble young lambs, they peck out their eyes and tear their mouths and tongues. For this cruelty—which is considerable, but nothing to our own—they are abominated.

Here is something a crow did. One morning three brown falcons were hooning around and wildly diving at every living thing, including a colossal pelican many times their size. It seemed likely they were just enjoying the general commotion their antics were creating, but they must have had a serious purpose because eventually one rose from the banks of a small island with a little egret in its claws. The other two flew off with it to share the meal.

A dozen galahs went back to the dead tree in the middle of the lake where they nest and camp at night. Two others sat lookout on the branch of another tree, 300 metres away; and a metre from the two galahs sat a crow—talking to them. Not cawing—talking, in a low and irate voice.

It was still talking when one of the falcons returned, flying at great speed towards the tree where the dozen galahs had settled. The crow took off in hot pursuit, surging to a level a few metres higher than the other bird and then, as the falcon's approach panicked the galahs into the air, the crow dived and knocked it sideways. The falcon recovered its poise, but the crow struck again and again and drove it off the lake. The crow flew back to the two galahs.

Absurd as it may seem, I could only see the crow's behaviour as fulfilment of an undertaking he had given the galahs. It was conscious philanthropy. Later, it also seemed to me to be the antithesis of our ancient belief, alive still in such fables as that of the fox and the scorpion, that animals cannot act outside their (savage) natures. Not for nothing is that view—and that fable— very popular with devotees of the free market.

A couple of weeks after the episode on the lake, I noticed a teal labouring on foot between two dams, when out of nowhere a falcon swept in to kill it. A millisecond before the falcon reached the helpless duck a crow reached the falcon and knocked it to the ground. Another crow followed up. Feathers flew. The duck fled back the way it had come. The falcon went home defeated. The crows hopped off into some cypresses. It was impossible to see what they had gained from the action, unless it had satisfied some charitable instinct or a subjective loathing for the other bird.

> Then I could fuse my passions into one clear stone
> And be simple to myself as the bird is to the bird.

Some birds, maybe, but not quite as the crow is to the crow. Or the magpie is to the magpie. Or the butcherbird with the beguiling song is to the butcherbird with the habits of a fiend. As I stood under a tree one day, a silvereye dropped at my feet. I took it in my hand and, as its chest heaved up and down, I looked up into the tree from which it had fallen. In the lowest branch a butcherbird was sitting, staring down at me and at the bird he had dropped. A butcherbird would fit in a beer glass, but that stare stood my hair on end. And as it stared, the silvereye's heart stopped beating.

Since then I've looked at many photos of butcherbirds, and none of them has a stare like that. The stare was that bird's and that moment's alone.

And then there is the kookaburra, the larrikin icon of Australia before Steve Irwin replaced it. *Laugh, kookaburra, laugh*, we used to sing. We have in the family a sequence of three photographs of a kookaburra perched in typical fashion on a fence. In the first you can see it has something large in its beak. In the second there is less of the thing. By the third, all that protrudes are a couple of webbed feet on scrawny legs. It's a duckling, a couple of weeks old. If they'd shown that before the Movietone News, this country might have a different view of itself.

Epsilon

Tony Wilson

We found him at the pound in the second week of April 2006. It was my soon-to-be-wife, Tamsin, who spotted him. He was a kelpie–heeler cross, maybe four to six months old, with a predominantly black face and a grey blaze running the length of his nose.

He was a bouncy thing. Every time we approached he'd leap with excitement, and then wag his way to the front of the cage to press his flanks through the wire. We'd pat with fingers and thumbs, the only way we could, and he'd drum his approval with his tail. When we left, he'd retreat slowly to the back of the cage, those awful cages with their hose-down concrete floors and inevitable piles of shit. If we returned after visiting other dogs, he'd forget our infidelity and charge forward for another pat.

We were sure everybody would want him.

We rang at 9.01 a.m. on the Monday he became available. When we got him, it felt like we'd won TattsLotto.

A day or two later, we collected him and the vet told us that he'd nearly failed his personality test, and was almost put down. 'You're going to have your hands full with that one,' he said.

A tough-looking woman in a flannelette shirt presented us with forms about desexing and registration. She scratched the dog's chin and cooed doggy love and ignored us completely while we signed the papers. Eventually she spoke.

'Are you two planning to have children?'

We were so taken aback, neither of said anything.

She ploughed on, undaunted. 'It's just that I see a lot of couples like you, in their thirties, who want kids and so try things out with a dog. Then they have kids and guess who suffers? Guess who ends up *back in here*.'

She was glaring at us. Our new dog was looking at us too, although less accusingly.

'We'll be good pet owners,' Tam said, which was better than I could muster. 'We know it's a commitment.'

The woman seemed suspicious, but further discussion was beyond the bounds of even her prodigious rudeness. Besides, he was ours. We had the adoption papers.

And so he came home with us. He was so petrified of the car on that first drive that he had to be nursed in the back by Tam.

His first meal was fresh chicken, and I had to wrestle his hind quarters to the ground to stop the vertical leaping and achieve something approaching a sit.

We put down newspaper and built barricades—tables, chairs, rolled-up carpets, cabinets, and other assorted obstacles—to keep him in the back room. His dog bed was tucked behind the set of *Les Misérables*.

He was out within thirty seconds.

We rebuilt the barricades, taller, wider.

We laid in bed, pet owners at last, listening, wondering if the barricades would hold. Two minutes later, we had our answer. *Pdd, pdd, pdd, pdd, pdd.* The tiny padding of paws on carpet.

He slept outside our room that first night.

....

We called him Charley Dog, after the character in Looney Tunes. The one who says, 'Oh boy, I'm gonna have a piazza. I'm gonna have a piazza!' We spelled it Charley with an 'ey' because we thought that's how it was spelled in the cartoon. As it happens, it's just regular 'Charlie' with an 'ie'. But it took seven years to find this out. By then we'd already engraved the dog tag.

The other jokey name we had for him was 'Epsilon'. This was because the rude woman at the pound had been partly right. We *did* plan to have children. In fact Tam was pregnant with our first baby *twenty-five days* after we took Charley home. So even as Charley enjoyed the beam of our combined attentions—two walks per day, liver treats, puppy school, dog clubs, cooked meals, social outings, regular bones, Christmas presents, there was a sense that competition was coming. 'We're Alpha and Beta,' we'd joke as we scratched his ears. 'And the kids will be Delta and Gamma. So you can be our little Epsilon. *You're a good little Epsilon!*'

When Polly was born, we fussed over the introduction like the impeccable dog owners we were. I dragged a baby jumpsuit home from the hospital to allow Charley to smell it. When the baby followed, he welcomed it in his Charley Dog way. An occasional sniff, a very occasional foot lick. We could call him off getting too close, as we could call him off anything.

That was the joy of the young Charley. He was so trainable, and so eager to please. What the vet had promised would be a handful was anything but. He had magnificent recall. He didn't dig holes or bark incessantly. He was great around food, always waiting to be invited. He didn't chew things. He was well behaved with other dogs. Even cats! He once set off after a possum at the park and Tam called him off, just as he was flinging himself into the tree. Charley pulled up and stared at her, as if to say, 'Oh, you're kidding, that is *not fair.*' But he copped it. He always copped it.

Charley was a magnificent Delta.

He was a magnificent Epsilon too. Our second baby was a boy, Harry, arriving in 2009. This time, Charley didn't get baby clothes to sniff. No warning at all that another pale, shrieking bundle of human was wriggling in on his hard-won territory.

Breastfeeding and toddler wrangling dominated Tam's days, so I'd take Charley to the Abbotsford Convent, where I had a writing studio. I'd ride the 5 kilometres there on the roads and he'd run on the footpath, learning within the space of weeks to stop at each side street, to wait for the shouted instruction, 'Cross.'

He'd sit under my feet all day, barely stirring. Then we'd ride and run the 5 kilometres home.

He was a super athlete, a loyal and loving pet. Polly adored throwing the tennis ball for him. Her first word was 'gog', short for Charley Dog.

He didn't deserve to become Zeta in 2011, with the arrival of Jack.

He absolutely didn't deserve to become Eta in 2015, with the arrival of Alice. When she arrived home, Charley just looked at me, as if to say, 'You've got to be fucking kidding. Another one.'

....

We now have four kids under ten. The third one, Jack, was born with severe cerebral palsy, which requires constant attention. Charley has his favourite spots in the house, watching the endless parades of shrieking mayhem with slowly blinking brown eyes. His coat is just that little greyer. His knees are too sore for tennis balls. He gets a pat when I guiltily think to myself that the day's almost over and I've forgotten to give him one. He doesn't seem to mind. I wonder if he remembers how Tam used to sauté offcuts and make doggy casseroles for him. Even with the seven-seater Tarago, we struggle to take him on outings with us. Prams and wheelchairs pile in the back. So often, there just isn't room.

The woman at the pound was right about this. The kids do overtake you.

I'll even tell this story. I know this is an animal book and 99 per cent of readers are barracking for the animals. But this actually happened, and I'm not proud of it. I'll only say by way of defence that I'm genetically predisposed to extreme bouts of vagueness. Famously, my mum left my newborn sister in the greengrocer's when she was five weeks old. A few minutes into the drive home, she had her frantic realisation and returned to see a large Greek man on the footpath, staring bewilderedly into the middle distance, nursing a baby against his apron.

My story is nowhere near as bad as that.

It happened on the day of my A-League commentary debut. I was sidelines reporter for Francis Leach on ABC Radio and had spent the hours beforehand nervously swotting up on jersey numbers and formations. I'd done some of this with the three older kids at the park, some on the train, and the rest prior to kick-off, pacing the media zone on the sideline.

At the start of the second half, with Melbourne Victory leading the Central Coast 2–1, my phone buzzed. It was a text from Tam.

Weird question I know but Charley Dog not here—Did you take him ...?

I was on the sidelines of an A-League game at Etihad Stadium. Did I take the dog! My stomach lurched with panic.

'*No!*' I texted back.

Francis asked me down the line for an opinion about the fitness of the Central Coast striker. I garbled something, but all my thoughts were on the dog. Where could he be? The last time I'd seen him was at the park, with three kids in tow, around 5.30 p.m., but he would have come home with us. Charley, abandoned as a puppy, never strayed further than 50 or so metres. Surely he came home with us. Unless … unless …

'Oh my god, Tam!' I said, making the call and attempting to speak into the phone with one side of my face as I listened for Francis's crosses with the other. 'Charley is at the park. I tied him to a park bench. I can't talk because I'm on air. But he's tied to a bench at the park!'

This is the bit where you're starting to judge me. You're picturing him watching us leave, attempting to follow, but being dragged back by the lead. You're hearing one or two plaintive whines, not barks because Charley would have figured he didn't need to bark—*It's not like they'd leave me here*, he'd have thought. *I'm one of the pack. They love me.* You're thinking about the three hours he spent next to that bench, as day became evening, as *They'll be back soon* became *They'll be back soon. Surely? Won't they?*

At home, Tam started ringing around to find somebody to watch the kids while she ran to the park. At the ground, I remembered the dog tag with my mobile phone number around Charley's neck. I checked for missed calls. There were two from unknown numbers. Again, I did the trick of phoning with one ear while listening for Francis's crosses with the other. *Oh shit, Leigh Broxham's warming up. Please don't cross to me now, Francis. Please!*

I dialled the unknown number. Hallelujah, it was a man at the park. Double hallelujah, he was still there with Charley. I whispered that I was commentating an A-League match, so couldn't chat, but asked if he could hang there for another couple of minutes because my wife was on her way. He said he could see a woman running towards the dog. I thanked him, restored my headset to position, took a deep breath, and did a bang-up job of enthusing about a Carl Valeri 360-degree turn that nearly produced goal of the season.

'*Got him,*' Tam texted.

'*Thank god. So sorry,*' I texted back.

'*He's furious. Hasn't wagged at all. Has sprinted straight for home.*'

Should I attempt to justify how it happened? How it was a perfect storm of carrying a disabled child, while pushing a swing, while answering a five year old's questions about bark? How I was trying to learn the Mariners' players' names? How it's so rare that we tie Charley up, but there were so many kids in the playground …

Are you willing to cut me some slack?

Would the woman at the pound be willing to cut me some slack?

Because Charley was. He was there wagging at the gate when I arrived home.

Gee Gee v GG

Tony Wright

In the winter of 1975, aboard an ill-tempered pony named Rami, I came within a short half-head of changing Australian history.

We, the pony and I, very nearly performed manslaughter upon the governor-general, Sir John Kerr.

It was not deliberate. I blame a hare.

You need quite a few unexpected elements to collide if you are to become party to what might have been interpreted as the assassination of a vice regal. I was between jobs; washed up as a bush journalist at the age of twenty-four, adrift in the national capital, Canberra.

Canberra is an unusual sort of place. It's judged by its isolation: an hour from the Hume Highway, a couple of hours from the coast, more hours from the capitals of Victoria and New South Wales. All because an argument between the pumped-up chests of Melbourne and Sydney needed to be settled.

All sorts of interesting characters have been bunched together in this outlying city ever since it was built. You might run into a prime minister in a shopping centre, though Gough Whitlam was busy trying to hold together a disintegrating government in mid 1975.

It was the year I met the family of the butler from Government House, Yarralumla.

His name was Bryan, and he was a large and loud Welshman who'd butled for the royal family before finding his way to the colonies and marrying a woman who already had seven children.

It struck me as bizarre to know someone who was butler to a governor-general, but it seemed to be unexceptional in Canberra.

Somehow, being between jobs and short of cash for things like food, I got into the habit of arriving at the family's home each day in time for dinner. I'm not sure the huge family even quite knew I was there sometimes.

One of the seven children was a young woman who had out-grown her enthusiasm for horses. Her passion that year was the guitar.

Learning that I had been brought up on a farm, she enquired whether I could ride a horse.

It happened that my father was a horseman and had presented me with my first pony when I was three.

My new friend explained that she owned a horse that hadn't been ridden for a while. She wanted to sell it but felt it might need a little work first, just to gentle it after its idle spell.

Would I take it for a ride each day until it was sale-fit?

Why not? I had time to spare and perhaps something to prove.

This being Canberra, the horse wasn't grazing in any old paddock.

It was stabled at Government House. Bryan the butler had made the arrangements.

There are those unkind enough to say Canberra is a good sheep paddock spoiled, and Government House, which sits on what was a splendid sheep station, has kept a decent-sized paddock for visitors to imagine what might have been and for vice regals to groove on: 54 hectares; or 133 acres, in the language sheep-station owners used. No sheep these days, though a mob of kangaroos hops lazily from the shelter of one tree to another.

And so, for a couple of weeks in June 1975, I drove my car out to Government House, where a kind policeman opened the gate to the servants' entrance and tipped his cap, and I was free to drive around to the stables that stood behind the stately vice-regal residence. No one ever asked for identification. Bryan's name was my password. Such days were they.

Rami was a little grey gelding with an evil eye. He pricked his ears and turned his head and measured me with that eye at my first approach, too much white showing around its dark depths.

Still, he allowed me to brush him down, get the bridle on him and the bit in his mouth, and he only shivered as the saddle went on and the girth tightened. But those ears moved back.

He'd been scamming. As I got my boot in the stirrup, about to swing aboard, Rami snapped his head around and tried to take a bite out of my leg, teeth bared. He couldn't quite accomplish it, but I should have known what was coming.

As I sank into the saddle, Rami's ears flattened and he put his head between his front legs. Squealing, he took to pig-rooting and bucking and trying to get my weight off him and into the dirt. He would have done it, too, but he turned out to be a bolter.

His bucking stopped as swiftly as it had begun and we took off across 133 acres that were supposed to ease the spirits of those burdened with ceremonially heading up a nation.

Rami wasn't much bigger than a pony, but he could gallop. There comes a moment when a horse's gait changes from a canter to a gallop and it is like changing gear to overdrive. Everything smooths out and there is only the sense of urgent power beneath you, the song of wind mixing with hoofbeats.

The problem was that Rami would not answer to the rein. He would not turn or slow however I sawed at his mouth.

No horse can bolt for long. The lungs and the heart won't support the stress of it.

And so it turned out with Rami. He slowed to a canter, kicked his heels a bit and calmed down until I could hold him and turn him and scold him, and eventually walk him back to the stable and towel off his sweat.

We built a morning ritual. Day after skittish day.

Rami would allow me to saddle him, and he'd buck and bolt with me clinging on until he'd simmer down and let me work him.

Each day, Rami's theatrics got a little shorter, a little less determined.

He still had the evil eye, and I never quite trusted him or lost my uneasiness. But I couldn't walk away and tell a girl whose stepfather was my daily key to the most exclusive address in the nation that I had failed to handle her horse.

Just as I began fooling myself that Rami and I were reaching an understanding and that the governor-general's green fields were my personal domain, I learned the truth.

On a particularly cold morning, with frost on the grass, Rami had performed his introductory snorting and pig-rooting and we were sailing across the old sheep paddock when I knew we were headed for trouble.

I spotted it before Rami, which allowed me half a heartbeat to get myself balanced and my boots hard into the stirrups.

Squatting behind a tussock was a hare. With Rami thundering towards it, the hare jumped and sprinted, dodging.

And Rami went mad.

Mid-stride the little horse plunged, altered course and found new energy. He picked up speed and was instantly further out of control than even on that first day.

Worse, we were running out of paddock.

Rami headed directly towards the old three-storey mansion that is the governor-general's residence.

And right out the front, on the ceremonial lawn, a lonely figure strolled, hands behind his back. A shock of pure white hair capped a recognisable head. Sir John Kerr, Governor-General of Australia, was taking a morning constitutional. Perhaps he was walking off his customary hangover. Bryan had let slip that Sir John was a fierce piss artist.

Neither the hare-addled Rami nor the queen's sot appeared to have any cognisance that we were all on a high-speed collision course.

Still at full gallop, Rami was just metres from mowing down His Excellency Sir John Kerr, former Chief Justice of the Supreme Court of New South Wales, currently the eighteenth Governor-General of Australia, when I began bellowng.

'Lookout lookout lookout!' I cried.

Sir John stopped, raised his head and looked with astonishment as a berserk horse and a rider barely clinging on rushed by, almost tearing the buttons from his cardigan.

I booted Rami to keep him going, performing an arc around the great house, storming him towards the stables. I tore the bridle and saddle from him, locked him away and took to my car.

I never looked back.

Rami was sold, and I trust he went to someone who enjoyed excitement. Sir John Kerr lived to dismiss the government of Gough Whitlam, who might never have forgiven me if he'd known I'd shouted a warning that had saved the life of the governor-general only five months previously.

I married the sister of the girl who owned Rami, and I returned to journalism.

In time, I attended receptions, dinners and garden parties as a guest of other governors-general. The stables had been torn down by then, but I never lost the urge to wander around and remember the day a mad little horse and I almost changed Australian history.

Biographies

Phillip Adams AO, FAHA is a broadcaster, writer and film-maker. He has presented *Late Night Live* for twenty-six years. He has written more than twenty books, and his work has appeared in scores of Australian newspapers and journals, the London *Times* and *The New York Times*. His many films include *The Adventures of Barry McKenzie*, *The Getting of Wisdom*, *Don's Party*, *Lonely Hearts* and *We of the Never Never*. Phillip has chaired the Australian Film Institute, the Australian Film Commission, Film Australia, the Commission for the Future, the National Australia Day Council and the Advisory Board of the Centre for the Mind at Sydney University and the Australian National University. As well as two Orders of Australia, Phillip was Australian Humanist of the Year (1987), Republican of the Year 2005, and received the Longford Award, the film industry's highest accolade, in 1981, the year he was appointed Senior Anzac Fellow. He received the Henry Lawson Arts Award (1987) and in 1998 the National Trust elected him one of Australia's 100 Living National Treasures. He has six honorary doctorates and was appointed to the Media Hall of Fame in 2014. A minor planet was named 'Phillip Adams' by the International Astronomical Union in 1997.

Greg Baum has been a journalist for almost forty years, mostly covering sport. He is presently chief sports columnist and associate editor at *The Age*. He has always lived in Melbourne. He has only ever owned one dog outright, but has been exposed to many others in a blended family environment.

Tony Birch is the author of five books: *Shadowboxing* (2006), *Father's Day* (2009), *Blood* (2011), *The Promise* (2014) and *Ghost River* (2015). He is currently the Bruce MacGuinness Research Fellow in the Moondani Balluk Academic Unit at Victoria University.

John Birmingham has published lots of books, most of them with his dog sitting under the desk, gently farting. He won the National Award for Non-Fiction with *Leviathan: an Unauthorised Biography of Sydney*. Then he started writing airport novels because they were more fun. His most recent series of books that improve with altitude are the Dave Hooper novels. You can join his book club and get a free story at jbismymasternow.com.

Anson Cameron had his first collection of short stories, *Nice Shootin Cowboy*, published in 1998. The title story was made into a short film a decade later. He has written six novels, and an acclaimed second collection of short stories, *Pepsi Bears*. *Boyhoodlum*, a memoir of his childhood in Shepparton, was published last year.

He has written for *The Bulletin*, *The Drum*, and currently writes a regular column for Fairfax.

Les Carlyon was born in northern Victoria into a family steeped in racing and horses. He began his journalistic career with Melbourne's *Sun News-Pictorial* and has been editor of *The Age*, editor-in-chief of the Herald and Weekly Times group and has lectured in journalism. He has won the Walkley Award and the Graham Perkin Australian Journalist of the Year and wrote the critically acclaimed and popular military histories *Gallipoli* and *The Great War*. But his first love is horse racing, on which he has written for almost fifty years.

John Clarke is a writer and performer, known for twenty-seven years of interviews with Bryan Dawe on ABC television, for *The Games*, for Fred Dagg and for various movies including *Death in Brunswick*. For some reason he has also written some books. He is twenty-seven.

Greg Combet is known for public roles as the leader of the Australian Council of Trade Unions and as a Labor government minister. He has been a key player in several high-profile issues: the 1998 waterfront dispute, the fight to recover the entitlements of former Ansett employees, obtaining compensation for victims of James Hardie asbestos products, leading the campaign against the Howard government's WorkChoices laws, and delivering Labor's carbon pricing and renewable energy legislation. Less well known is that his public life has been underpinned by knowledge and experience gained growing up at a winery, as a mining engineer, union activist, superannuation trustee, bank director, industrial negotiator and advocate, politician, communicator and campaigner. He was awarded a Member of the Order of Australia in 2006, and published *The Fights of My Life* in 2014. Following two terms in parliament, he is now pursuing a career in the superannuation industry and the private sector. He is a director of IFM Investors, ME Bank, advises Industry Super Australia and does consulting work.

Trent Dalton writes for *The Weekend Australian Magazine*. He has twice won a Walkley Award for excellence in journalism, been a four-time winner of the national News Awards Feature Journalist of the Year Award, and was named Queensland Journalist of the Year in 2011. His journalism has twice been nominated for a United Nations of Australia Media Peace Award. In 2014 and 2013, he was named Best Feature journalist at the annual Kennedy Awards for excellence in New South Wales journalism. His writing includes several short and feature-length film screenplays. His first short film, *Silencer*, was a finalist at the annual Tropfest Australia short film festival. He was nominated for a 2010 AFI Best Short Fiction screenplay award for his short film *Glenn Owen Dodds*, starring David Wenham. It won the International Prix Canal award at the Clermont-Ferrand International Short Film Festival in France, and Dalton was named Best Writer at Aspen Shortsfest 2010. His latest feature film screenplay, *Home*, is a love story inspired by his 2011 non-fiction collection *Detours: Stories from the Street*, the culmination of three months immersed in Brisbane's homeless community.

Robert Drewe's novels, short stories and memoirs—including *The Drowner, Our Sunshine, The Shark Net* and *The Bodysurfers*—have won national and international prizes, been widely translated, and been adapted for film, television, radio and theatre around the world.

John Elder is a Melbourne-based writer and ornithologist. He's currently completing a novel about poetry and disrupted childhood for his daughters, and a non-fiction book about birds and the meaning of the meaning of life.

Jonathan Green is a writer, editor and broadcaster, who rides when he can.

John Harms is the energy behind www.footyalmanac.com.au. He recently worked with Michelle Payne on her autobiography, *Life as I Know It*. A Queenslander, he lives in Melbourne with Susan and their young family. He doesn't get to Fraser Island enough.

Malcolm Knox is the author of more than twenty books and has been a journalist at *The Sydney Morning Herald* since 1994. He grew up with beagles, survived without a dog for many years, but settled down with a blue heeler–kelpie cross called Bruce.

Garry Linnell can recall that when he started in journalism in the 1980s, he had hair. He has covered Olympic Games, football, cricket tours and written several books. He has also edited various newspapers and *The Bulletin* magazine and worked in commercial television. He is now a radio broadcaster in Sydney. He misses his days as a junior footballer in Geelong, a career he embellishes at every opportunity.

William McInnes is an award-winning actor and author. He lives in Melbourne with his two children and Ray and Delilah, two lovely kelpies as silly as wheels.

Shaun Micallef is an Australian comedian who has appeared in many TV shows (*Shaun Micallef's Mad as Hell*, *The Ex-PM* and *Talkin' 'Bout Your Generation*), films (*Aquamarine*, *Bad Eggs* and

Fitzcarraldo) and also written a few things (*Preincarnate, Black Beauty* and *February Dragon* by Colin Thiele).

Bruce Pascoe is a Yuin, Bunurong and Tasmanian man and lives at Mallacoota in Far East Gippsland. He has published thirty-one books and was editor and publisher of *Australian Short Stories* magazine for sixteen years and sixty-five issues. In 2000 he won The Australian Literature Award for his novel *Shark* and in 2013 he won the Prime Minister's Award for his YA novel *Fog a Dox*, and in 2016 won the NSW Premier's Book of the Year Award for the history *Dark Emu: Black Seeds*.

Liam Pieper's books include *The Feel-Good Hit of the Year*, short-listed for the National Biography Award, and *Mistakes Were Made*, a short collection of essays. He was co-recipient of the 2014 M Literary Award, and was the inaugural creative resident of the UNESCO City of Literature of Prague, where he completed his first novel, *The Toymaker*, which is available now.

Frank Robson is a well-known journalist and author. He has won two Walkley Awards for feature writing, and has worked for a range of publications here and overseas, including *TIME* and *The Sydney Morning Herald*.

Andrew Rule grew up in eastern Victoria surrounded by animals. Too small to be a mounted policeman, too big to be a jockey, too frightened to be a rodeo rider, he won the 1974 Sale Agricultural Show essay competition (first prize $5) before starting as a reporter with the *Gippsland Times* and *Maffra Spectator*. He later worked at *The Age, The Herald* and the *Herald Sun*, has written and published several books and claims to have once spent a week with a circus. He has variously maintained three terriers, two cats and too many old ponies and slow racehorses.

John Silvester has been a crime reporter in Melbourne since 1978, first with *The Sun News-Pictorial* then with *The Sunday Age* and *The Age*. He worked for *The Sunday Times Insight* team in London in 1990 and has co-authored many true crime books, including *The Silent War, Leadbelly* and the *Underbelly* series. He admits harbouring several dogs, including a three-legged Jack Russell terrier.

Jeff Sparrow is a writer, editor and broadcaster. He's the immediate past editor of *Overland*, he contributes a fortnightly column to the *Guardian* and he appears daily on 'Breakfasters' on 3RRR.

Paul Toohey is a senior reporter for News Corp Australia. He has won three Walkley Awards and the Graham Perkin Journalist of the Year. He lives in Darwin.

Don Watson's most recent books are *The Bush* (Hamish Hamilton) and *Worst Words* (Vintage). He lives in Melbourne.

Tony Wilson has written for both children and adults for more than a decade. His satirical novels for adults include *Players* (2005) and *Making News* (2010) and he's penned features for *The Age*, *The Monthly* and *Good Weekend*. His most recent release is *The Selwood Boys* books for middle-grade kids—a fictionalised childhood for the four footballing brothers. His picture book, *The Cow Tripped over the Moon*, is shortlisted for CBCA Book of the Year 2016. Tony also curates and maintains the Speakola website, which promotes great speeches, famous and otherwise.

Tony Wright has been a journalist since 1970, when he began a cadetship at the tri-weekly *Portland Observer* in far south-west Victoria, where he had been raised on farms. He has written for numerous publications in the forty-six years since, apart from a hiatus in 1975, when, after a brush with a pony and a governor-general, he became a rock'n'roll roadie and sound mixer. He has been a senior writer for *The Canberra Times*, *The Sydney Morning Herald* and *The Bulletin* and is currently National Affairs Editor of *The Age*. Wright has written two plays and two bestselling books, was named Magazine Feature Writer of the Year twice, has won several UN Media Peace Prizes, a Quill Award and has been a Walkley Awards finalist five times.

More great titles from MUP

Comeback
The Fall and Rise of Geelong
James Button

ISBN 9780522866155 (pb)
ISBN 9780522866162 (ePub)

One town. One football club. One struggle for greatness.

James Button fell in love with the Geelong Football Club as a boy. It was a family affair. But as the years wore on and the defeats mounted, one nagging question became louder and louder: would his team ever win a premiership again?

Comeback tells the Geelong story—how a town unloved by the big city up the road turned to football to show it was as good as anyone.

It paints the characters—two Gary Abletts, 'Polly' Farmer, Bob Davis, 'Bomber' Thompson, Matthew Scarlett, Joel Selwood and many others—who helped to make Geelong a byword for excitement, and it explains how a bunch of talented but flashy individuals ended years of despair by finding the magic ingredient that makes a great team. More than a book about sport, *Comeback* shows how the history of a town and the spirit of a place can be funnelled through the fortunes of a football club.

James Button was an *Age* journalist and speechwriter to former prime minister, Kevin Rudd. His 2012 book *Speechless: A Year in My Father's Business*, was short-listed for the National Book Industry Book of the Year, the National Biography Award, the Walkley Award and the Melbourne Prize.

BOOKS WITH SPINE
www.mup.com.au

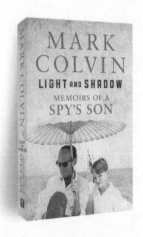

Light and Shadow
Memoirs of a Spy's Son
Mark Colvin

ISBN 9780522870893 (pb)
ISBN 9780522870909 (ePub)

Mark Colvin is a broadcasting legend. He is the voice of ABC Radio's leading current affairs program *PM*.

He was a founding broadcaster for the groundbreaking youth station Double J; he initiated *The World Today* program; and he's one of the most popular and influential journalists in the twittersphere.

Mark has been covering local and global events for more than four decades. He has reported on wars, royal weddings and everything in between. In the midst of all this he discovered that his father was an MI6 spy.

Light and Shadow is the incredible story of a father waging a secret war against communism during the Cold War, while his son comes of age as a journalist during the tumultuous Whitlam and Fraser years and embarks on the risky career of a foreign correspondent.

Mark was witness to some of the most world-changing events, including the Iranian hostage crisis, the buildup to the first Gulf War in Iraq and the direct aftermath of the shocking genocide in Rwanda. But when he contracted a life-threatening illness while working in the field, his life changed forever. Mark Colvin's engrossing memoir takes you inside the coverage of major news events and gently navigates the complexity of his father's double life.

MUP
BOOKS WITH SPINE
www.mup.com.au

Press Escape
Shaun Carney

ISBN 9780522870022 (pb)
ISBN 9780522870039 (ePub)

Getting away was always a driving ambition for Shaun Carney—from an outer-suburban house in the 60s and 70s, from a family with a secret: a father with a double life and a borrowed name.

Journalism gave Shaun that escape, to another life, to becoming a different person. For 34 years he took every opportunity it offered, flourished and knew success even while dealing with the personal struggle of his own child battling cancer. But a greater sense of freedom came when he forgave the people he'd wanted to flee and, unexpectedly, let go of the life that he'd worked so hard to create. In this beautifully crafted memoir one of Australia's leading political journalists writes movingly about discovering the one story that really matters.

Shaun Carney has been a journalist, editor and columnist with *The Herald*, *The Age* and the *Herald Sun*. He is an adjunct associate professor with the School of Social Sciences at Monash University.

MUP
BOOKS WITH SPINE
www.mup.com.au

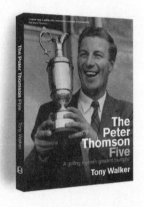

The Peter Thomson Five
A Golfing Legend's Greatest Triumphs
Tony Walker

ISBN 9780522869118 (pb)
ISBN 9780522869200 (ePub)

On the 51st anniversary of his last open championship, Peter Thomson talks about his life, golf and how he achieved Open glory.

Peter Thomson won five golf Open Championships. He is only the third golfer to have won five or more, behind the great Harry Vardon, who won six. It is a feat unlikely to be repeated in the modern era and puts him in the legendary league of sports players like Don Bradman, Rod Laver, Margaret Court and Dawn Fraser.

Tony Walker is a golf tragic who has spent his career as a foreign correspondent and a political editor for various Fairfax papers. He has won two Walkley awards and was awarded the Centenary Medal for contributions to journalism in 2001. He is an adjunct professor at LaTrobe University in the School of Communications. He has written a biography of Yasser Arafat. A frustrated sports journalist, this is his first sporting book.

MUP
BOOKS WITH SPINE
www.mup.com.au

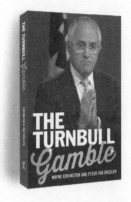

The Turnbull Gamble

Wayne Errington and
Peter van Onselen

ISBN 9780522866155 (pb)
ISBN 9780522866162 (ePub)

The Liberal Party took a risk replacing Tony Abbott with Malcolm Turnbull.
They had seen how voters could turn when the ALP tore down a first-term
prime minister. But MPs were desperate, having witnessed the collapse in
polling during Abbott's prime ministership. By the time Turnbull called the
election it was still unclear what he wanted to achieve. He seemed strangely
underprepared for a job that he had fought so long to win.

Turnbull leads a party whose culture he doesn't share. While the narrow election
victory may have justified the gamble to place him in office, does Turnbull have
the leadership qualities needed to break the cycle of division and instability of
the last decade?

Wayne Errington is Associate Professor in Politics and Associate Dean
(Learning and Teaching) in the Faculty of Arts at Adelaide University.

Peter van Onselen is Contributing Editor at *The Australian* and a presenter at
Sky News. He is a professor in politics at the University of Western Australia.

Together they wrote the bestsellers *John Winston Howard: The Definitive
Biography* and *Battleground: Why the Liberal Party Shirtfronted Tony Abbott*.

MUP
BOOKS WITH SPINE
www.mup.com.au